MY MUM AND ME

MESSAGES FROM BEYOND THE GRAVE

KIM KNIGHT

G Publishing Partners, LLC

ALSO BY KIM KNIGHT

UNSOLVED MYSTERIES SERIES

The Note

The Red Light Girls

'Til Death Do Us Part

STANDALONE BOOKS

Sacrifices

NONFICTION WORKS

My Mum and Me

BLURB

Want to read more by Kim Knight?
Click here to sign up for the newsletter.
www.subscribepage.com/authorkimknight

"Life after death is no longer a 'possibility' for me, it's a reality. It was proven within seventy-two hours of Mum passing away."

Is there such a thing as life after death?

If you've been looking for confirmation that the soul of a deceased person lives on, this memoir will provide all the proof you need. Experience a life changing story—a loss of a mother who was overseas at the time of her passing, and how she found her way back to her daughter within seventy-two hours of her being pronounced dead, then made her visit from the spirit realm unquestionably known to her daughter here on Earth, in time and space.

A Memoir: My Mum and Me
Messages From Beyond the Grave
COPYRIGHT©2021
KIM KNIGHT
Cover Design by Wren Taylor

This book is a work of fiction. The names, characters, places, and incidents are the products of the author's imagination or are used fictitiously. Any resemblance to actual events, business establishments, locales, or persons, living or dead, is entirely coincidental.

All rights reserved. No part of this publication may be reproduced, stored in a retrieval system, or transmitted in any form or by any means (electronic, mechanical, photocopying, recording, or otherwise) without the prior written permission of both the copyright owner and the publisher. The only exception is brief quotations in printed reviews.

The scanning, uploading, and distribution of this book via the Internet or any other means without the permission of the publisher is illegal and punishable by law.

Please purchase only authorized electronic editions, and do not participate in or encourage electronic piracy of copyrighted materials. Your support of the author's rights is appreciated.

Published in the United States of America by:

DLG Publishing Partners
San Antonio, TX 78217
www.DLGPublishingPartners.com

The publisher does not have any control over and does not assume any responsibility for author or third-party websites or their content.

This is probably the most important and biggest thing I've written in my career as a writer to date.

I fully dedicate every word of this memoir to my beautiful, strong, and hard-working mum Viv, who even seems to be working hard in spirit to let me know she's watching over me and approves of this memoir of my most life-changing experience to date. You were always a 'super woman' to me, and you still show me you are from the other side!

Enjoy your next incarnation! I hope to meet you again someday, but until then, just as I promised you, I will keep writing, and will stay open to your communication.

Thank you for your approval of this memoir.

To all the spiritually gifted people who walk this Earth as humans. Your role here on Earth is so important, thank you.

CONTENTS

Chapter 1	1
Chapter 2	14
Chapter 3	16
Chapter 4	21
Chapter 5	32
Chapter 6	41
Chapter 7	50
Chapter 8	59
Chapter 9	66
Chapter 10	83
A Note from the Author	87
About the Author	93

SNEAK PEEK OF THE NOTE

1. Sleeping Dogs, Wake	97
2. Money Talks	106
3. What's Done In The Dark	116
4. De ja Vu	122
5. One Step Ahead	130
6. I Spy	138

SNEAK PEEK OF SACRIFICES

1. Memories	143
2. Farewell	147
3. It's A New Dawn, A New Day	158
4. Maurice's Place	163
5. If You Could Do It Again	174
6. Hopeful	187

1

AND SO IT BEGINS

THE PURPOSE of me writing this memoir is not to convince you there's life after death, or that we don't just die and that's it. The reason is simply to reassure you that yes, without a shadow of a doubt, my friend, there's life after death. I have evidence to confirm it, and I hope my direct exchange with the spirit realm's communication, will sooth and calm you. It's my sincere wish and hope that once you close the pages of the short memoir, you're less worried about anyone you've lost or are about to lose.

I wish to share my story and first-hand experience of communication, from beyond the grave, with you. I don't wish to bog you down with the fine details of my mum's passing, firstly, because it's probably not what you want to hear. Secondly, Mum was a private person, so private, my sisters and I never learned she was dying until the eleventh hour. Lastly, I'm not really in the business of writing books that pull on one's heart-strings and makes people reach for the tissues, unless it's a fictional romantic suspense or some kind of a thriller.

Now, I'm not trying to sell you a sob story over my mum's transition from here in time and space on Earth, to the ancestral realm. Instead, I'm here to open your mind to the possibility of life after death, and show you once a person transitions, his or her soul does leave the body and it can and does have the ability to communicate with those who were left behind, if the deceased individual so wishes.

In order to respect Mum and who she was as woman, a private person at times, I'll not bang on about how she went from a vibrant, happy, warm soul to a bed-bound woman with little control over her body.

No. Mum would not want me to focus on this as a way to sooth and assure you about the afterlife. She'd want me to focus on how she communicated with me, as well as pass on my cultural traditions of ancestor vibration to inspire you, and hopefully, so you may also connect with a loved one who has passed over—or will soon pass—without the need to use mediums, spiritual workers, or pay anyone.

As I write this chapter, it's been twelve days since Mum's passing at the ripe age of just seventy years old. I don't personally think this is old, especially when you take into consideration the person's quality of life before passing, and his or her overall general health.

Now, as I write this body and reflect, I don't even recall Mum so much as suffering from a cold, or ever being in hospital. She was fit, healthy, and very much in shape. She was always in the garden, an avid plant lover, and good with nature. Mum had 'a green finger' as they say. The thoughts and vivid pictures float through my mind's eye of Mum in her garden, make me smile.

On the 28th of January 2021, my intuition began to speak to me. Now, when she speaks—and she is a rather persistent *she*, I've learned in my thirty-eight years on this Earth, I better listen, so I did. And it's funny just not in 'haha funny' fashion, as I write this and glance through my journal entries, from that day to the present, only seven days before, on the 21st of January, I randomly signed up for an online webinar on non-fiction memoir writing.

Why the hell did I do that?

I can only put it down to two things. First, but a large one, the world-wide pandemic, Covid-19. Over the last year, the contagion has caused me to take all kinds of free and paid online courses to pass the time while cooped up in the house. Second, I have always loved to read memoirs, from rock stars to everyday people like me, I consume them all.

At the time, when I had signed up for the course, I thought, *maybe one day, I'll write about a time I did x, y, or z.* But I never imagined I would have evidence, solid, real personal evidence of life after death that would push me to write this short memoir.

Anyway, I'm going off topic. As I was saying, back to the 28th of January 2021.

My alarm went off as usual around six in the morning. As soon as it did, I opened my eyes in the darkness, and I stared up at the ceiling. I remember I had this overwhelming need to pray.

For whom, for what? At the time I didn't know.

I'm also not a religious person, meaning I don't subscribe to a religion. I don't own a bible. I don't go to church. However, I am deeply spiritual in nature. Therefore, I don't deny faith or religion, it's just not for me.

I have learned and studied all mainstream religions of the world. And I have a deep interest in them—all of them. I like to understand the perspectives of them, each and every one. In school, 'Religious Education' was a subject I enjoyed and excelled in.

The only reason I don't follow a religion today is because, my beliefs around life after death, reincarnation, and the soul's journey are, in a sense, dismissed by mainstream tradition.

What most mainstream religions advocate as what happens upon death, really does not resonate with me. I've always been drawn to the spirit realm —paranormal things. As a qualified astrologer, the idea of life incarnations when one looks at the topic from the perspective of an astrologer and study a person's birth chart, life after death just resonates better from this esoteric stance.

My beliefs align more with things like believing in the universe, Taoism, and, of course, Buddhist beliefs around reincarnation and karma. That said, I don't claim to be a strict follower of any of this. I just believe in spirituality as a whole, from a non-religious stance. Also, when we die, I fully believe it's not the end, if anything, it's the beginning.

I can now say after the death of my mum . . . Yes, the soul lives on. I was right all along to not subscribe to any form of religion which dismisses this. But now, people who do subscribe to a void of life after death, I have no problem with—with them or their faith.

I live and let live, I say.

Now, back to the six a.m. wake-up call. I got out

of bed, and I needed to do two things: one, get a hold of a large white pillar candle, and two, pray. So, I did I followed my intuition.

As the day progressed, the morning routine kicked in: shower, dress, home-school, and so on. But I felt the need to call my mum. We were due for a catch-up. But to be honest, during the Covid-19 pandemic, which is still in full swing at this point in January 2021, between home-schooling, running the house, and trying to write my fictional works that will release later in the year, I was whacked!

Time had somehow slipped away from me. *It has a way of doing that at times.*

Late morning, when I stopped the current home-school for a break, I had to call Mum, I just felt it. It wasn't as if I needed to call as it was overdue. No, it felt more like an urgency as if something was amiss, or wrong.

It was such a strange feeling back then, and it pushed me to make the call.

Break time could not come quick enough. Oh, and I also felt like I had to do a video call, not a normal voice one.

I must see Mum, not just hear her, I recalled thinking at the time.

Due to the pandemic and Mum's age, she was

seventy, phone calls within the family had become the main form of contact to shield her.

That day, she refused my video call. I was a little upset, but I shrugged it off and thought I'd call again later.

I sent a message her a simplistic message.

—*Hi, Mum.*
—*We need to catch up.*
—*I've not spoken to you in a while.*

Mum called me back immediately, using the video call feature. Glancing at the screen of my phone, the camera came up. I was over the moon to see her. However, as soon as the camera connected, and I saw my mum, I knew something was wrong.

She looks ill. Just by viewing her on screen, she seemed as if she was in a lot of pain. Her speech was slurred.

Did she have a slight stroke and not know?

I was panicking inside. But I tried to remain calm and not show I was upset. I didn't want to panic Mum just in case she was not aware she had possibly had a stroke.

It's conceivable. These things do happen.

I've heard it called a mini stroke. When it's so slight, the person is not aware. Also, I remembered how people who had suffered a stroke looked.

My Nanna, Mum's mum had a few before she had passed away.

As I studied Mum carefully but tried to not appear as if I was, she also looked like she had lost weight.

Mum's petite anyway. At around five-foot-three and a trim UK dress size twelve, it was easy to notice the weight loss due to her natural build.

Apart from Mum's physical appearance, as I glanced at the camera, I remembered saying playfully to her, *Mum it's after nine in the morning. What ya doin' in bed at this hour?*

She laughed, and so did I. But I was not laughing inside. No. I was worried.

Mum is never in bed at that time.

Even though she had retired years ago, she was always up by six in the morning.

She used to say to me, *My body clock just won't adjust now that I've stopped working.*

Mum was always up with the sunrise. And I guarantee on any normal day, by that hour of the morning, she had already done a load of washing, cleaned the house, and ran some errands.

On the weekend, and when she was on her way out, she'd wake me up with a video call. And yes, she'd be the one to ask me what I was doing in bed.

My mum was ill, I was sure of it. And I was

convinced she was trying to hide how sick she was, as well as how much pain she was in.

During that call, Mum had placed an arm over her head as she reclined back. It was almost as if she was trying to hide her hair from view.

I noticed this, and I said to myself—as I looked closer—*why is Mum's hair so short?*

Mum always had lovely hair. Why, I remember braiding it for her.

What's wrong, I had asked Mum outright. *Are you in pain?* I could see, as well as sense, she was.

True to form, Mum downplayed the whole thing.

Oh, just the usual aches and pains you get at my age, she had told me. *That's all.*

I was not buying that story. Like I had said prior, Mum was as-fit-as-a-fiddle, as they say, her health was never an issue. The only time I recalled Mum ever complaining of any problem was years ago. It was back when I was a teen and had something to do with her back.

But I could tell Mum was not suffering with just a backache—there was more to it, I was sure.

As I paid more attention to her, taking in every clue on the screen, her breathing came across as laboured, and each breath seemed like it was hard work for her.

Gently I applied the pressure again about her health.

But she remained mute and brushed me off. I changed the subject and started talking about the pandemic and all the people who had passed.

Mum thought I did not notice, but I did . . . a tear had welled in her right eye. It fell over the corner and slid down her cheek.

Now, I was stumped and wondered what I had said to upset her. I shut up immediately about the death toll.

She turned away, and I teared up. I know something was up at that point.

I stopped talking and listened attentively to the phone call that morning in January—the last video call I'd ever have with my mum.

I'm pending results from the hospital, she had told me. *For a Covid-19 test.*

I lost my shit internally when I heard this. At this point, I had so many questions over how she could have picked it up.

You see, Mum never left the house. She had the shopping delivered to her doorstep, and no one was allowed inside.

She brushed me off some more and stated, *it was probably from one of the delivery men. The ones who brought the food shopping over.*

I was stumped. Covid-19 of all things.

Mum is healthy, I had thought back then. *She's seventy. Age isn't on her side.*

This virus, as I continued to write this memoir, had still proven deadly for the old, and young alike.

Her breathing seemed hard again. And her slurred words came out as if it each one was painful to speak.

I was in a hurry to get off the phone to call my sister—to relay what I had seen and heard.

I love you, Mum, I had told her toward the end of the call. *Don't worry. The test will come back negative.*

Strategically, I tried to get more information about when she'd get the results. But Mum was so vague with me. Her speech was so slurred. And it appeared as though she could not fully recall the details herself, which was unlike her.

Once I hung up, I set out to ring my siblings.

My oldest sister never answered when I called. So, I left her a message, then called my middle sister. But there was no answer, so I left a message once again.

Tears welled in my eyes at that point, and I cried.

That morning, I had awakened with an eerie feeling—even had the notion something was up.

A strong push to pray had hit me, and I did not know what for.

Like I said, I'm not religious in that sense, but I did pray to the universe for everyone's well-being around the world, due the pandemic.

One of my sisters—the eldest—called me back.

Mum's not well, I told her. *She must get to the hospital. I think she's had a stroke. That's how she appeared to me. Her speech, it was—she looks in pain. Something's not right.*

My sister listened to me, silently, taking in each word I spoke. And then, she replied to me.

There's a lot you don't know about Mum's health, was her exact wording to me. *I only just found out about a month ago.*

My sister told me how Mum's silence was her trying to protect us. She had already undergone a positive Covid-19 test, and our uncle was also in isolation. Then, as if that wasn't enough of a bombshell, she delivered the final blow.

Mum has cancer, her words hit me hard. *She's been enduring medical treatments since January 2020.*

I'll be honest. I didn't think it could happen again in such a short amount of time. but yeah, it did. I literally lost my shit. But at this point, it was externally. I didn't hold it in.

No one told me, why? I remember demanding to know, but as it turned out, Mum had sworn my uncle to secrecy.

None of us were meant to know—especially me, that was her strictest orders.

My uncle, who was so close to Mum, *had found himself in between a rock and a hard place*. But, in the end, his loyalty remained with my mum.

I can only imagine this might have been out of fear that she would stop taking talking to him. So, no one had known what her state of health was except for him—to a degree.

How will she make it to the hospital for her treatments now? Fear rose up inside me.

He had been taking her for her to chemotherapy throughout 2020, all during the pandemic. And she picked up Covid-19 at the hospital on her last visit, sometime during January 2021.

Imagine how I felt. I was angry with the world.

Why did Mum withhold this information from me—from us all?

Once I had a tearful discussion with both my sisters, the conclusion came to me.

Mum felt she could beat the cancer and did not want to worry any of us.

She was a fighter, a survivor, who tore away from an abusive, unfaithful husband after more than ten years of marriage. Knowing Mum, she was prepared to war with her cancer, but that meant a solo battle.

2

WHEN LOVED ONES WITHDRAW

Mum was always a very private person, who never really liked to make a fuss over anything.

Still, I felt like I had been betrayed at first. That was until I really reflected on the situation, and who my mum really was as a person, as well as how the weeks leading up to her death went by.

I had a conversation with two really good friends of mine.

One agreed with how Mum handled it, and said she'd do the same. Reason being, she'd rather her loved ones not encounter pain, upset, and worry for a whole year. She'd prefer them experience the emotions in just a few weeks, rather than drawing it out and making the pain and heartache last a whole year, during a pandemic where one could not have reached a loved one in person, as in my case.

My other girlfriend also reasoned that it showed the strength of my mum, and how she really did not want to burden her kids.

I took in their points of views, and I saw some truth in both of them. Both theories applied to who Mum was as person, in many ways.

None the less, it was, and on some days still is, painful. But one thing I can testify to and maybe you can as well, when a loved one has a terminal illness or understands that they will die soon, they withdraw.

Like I said, Mum didn't want us to know about her illness, and decided not to tell a soul. Only my uncle knew, and from what I heard, even then, when he attended her appointments, she made him sit outside and wait.

Typical Mum, such a fighter and ready to do battle on her own.

I also see this as Mum withdrawing from us all, even her own brother.

3

THE UNTHINKABLE

A FEW DAYS after I found out Mum was ill, the unthinkable happened.

She had to go back into hospital, literally, within a few days of my last conversation with her. The one where she had told me she was waiting for her Covid-19 result.

Pneumonia. Covid-19. Cancer. It was a lot to take in.

At this point, my sisters and I had no idea what kind of cancer. Mum was like a brick wall. She would not tell us anything. In fact, Mum never even admitted she was sick with cancer. But she realised my sisters and I knew when she was admitted to the hospital again.

My oldest sister suspected lung cancer. During 2020, she had spent some time with Mum, and had to pick her up from an appointment. One my uncle could not make it to.

At the time, Mum never told my sister why she had gone to the hospital when she picked her up, well, not the real reason, anyway.

No. She brushed off my sister's enquiry with the infamous 'routine check-up' response. That's the impression my sister had given me. After a conversation with my sister while Mum was in hospital, she told me she had suspected cancer due to her cough, her pains, and her other symptoms.

When she picked her up from the hospital, Mum was in a bad way. This led her to suspect lung cancer. Now, she said she had asked Mum outright about her health. But as usual, Mum, the private person she was, had brushed my sister off.

Mum spent a little over a week in hospital. She had beat Covid-19 and a bad case of pneumonia.

I was so scared. It was the worst week of my life!

Each night, I'd ask the universe to give her another night, so I could wake up and call her in the morning.

Please allow her to hold on, I had pleaded back then. *Do not take her from me.*

She did hold on. Once we got the all clear, she was able to return home. Covid-19 was no longer a threat to anyone. Mum could not pass it on to anyone who cared for her. My heart had sung with joy.

But just because she was home, and she had beat Covid-19, didn't mean she'd open up. Nope, Mum withdrew. She refused to see her siblings, refused home healthcare and assistance, she basically refused aid from everyone but her children.

People who are soon to depart this incarnation, withdraw. It's part of the process of dying for them.

They reject food, drinks, visitors, and sometimes even shy away from all forms of communication.

Conversation is all I had with Mum due to travel restrictions, during the Covid-19 pandemic. I could not leave the country! I was in France. The boarders were closed, so that was the end of that. I could not go anywhere.

When a loved one who is dying withdraws, in my honest experience and from personal advice, please respect their wishes.

Clearly, medication was essential and something I would encourage anyone to take or help someone if needed. But if a person's not up to visiting, talking, or seeing people, it's probably best to not force the issue.

Respect how the individual feels because it's important. One thing I learnt about the withdrawal process was this . . . *Terminally ill people about to face death soon, desire to prepare for departure.*

What did it mean? Well, simply put, the individual not only prepared themselves to let go of their beloved—you—the person prepares you to let go of them as well—in physical body, at least.

This is why they withdraw.

It's natural to want to hold on to them, sit with them, and be there all the time.

Damn, imagine how I felt. I was overseas when all this happened. All I had were calls. Mum would not video call with me, just voice call.

Which was another thing I realised after reflection.

People who are dying, well, in Mum's case, at least, realise they don't look visually how they once did.

Mum's lovely hair had fallen out. She had lost weight, which she constantly complained about to me. Visually, she noticed the changes. She did not want anyone else to see this, especially me.

However, Mum's voice and accent remained the same.

It was hard to imagine she was dying. Some days, she was lucid in thought and speech, other days, she slurred and did not make sense, not fully, in her conversations.

Honestly, don't take it personally if your loved one withdraws. It's part of the process. Instead, cherish the time you have with this individual. Talk about anything and everything, don't dwell on negativity. But if you need to clear the air about conflict, do so with grace. For you may never get a second chance.

I never had any conflict to clear with Mum. It felt more like the conversations were times for us to bond. We talked about the future, a lot.

What are you doing? Mum had posed that question, among others. *What will you do? Where are you going? What's on your mind, today? Did I ever tell you . . .*

I understand this line of questioning. She had memories to depart with—things she felt the need to share. Personally, for me, I just wanted to hear her voice. To have nice conversations as basic as they were. It was all I had.

And now, I cherish every minute I spent with her. *Please, do the same.*

4

THE MEANING OF LIFE: DO WE EVER DIE?

LOOKING over my journal one afternoon, I asked myself, *what's the meaning of life? Do we ever truly die?* Science might never provide a satisfactory response, not one for me, anyway.

Once Mum arrived home from hospital stay, after she had beat Covid-19 and pneumonia, two things were clear. First, Mum's cancer was in fact lung cancer. It had travelled everywhere, aggressively to her brain, bones, and blood. Secondly, family had about three weeks left with her.

I started to question a lot of things. Why hadn't Mum said anything? How can things progress so quickly? And what really was the point and meaning of life—do we ever really die?

The bottom line to me at the time, she had undergone a year of treatment.

Lung cancer is so hard to treat.

A year was a long time according to the doctors. She had weeks, not months or years left with us. It was too aggressive.

Mum had beat Covid-19, but she could not beat the aggressive cancer.

I was pissed. The thought of Mum losing her memory, the ability to walk, and full control of her body, turned me upside down.

Once Mum arrived home, it was all about making her last weeks as comfortable as possible. Each day, I'd wake, and she'd be on my mind—every night also. My evenings were spent in reflection.

Slowly, she started to decline. First, her ability to walk, but Mum was on a mission to keep hold of her independence. So much so, she did not always let my sisters know when she needed to venture into the bathroom. She'd try to make her way to the commode, alone. And once, she had a serious fall. After that, one of my sisters basically refused to sleep. Each night, she'd keep watch and listen just in case Mum tried to move. And Mum being Mum, had refused assistance to make the trip to the commode. This kept my oldest sister awake all night.

From my daily calls with Mum, some days, she was so lucid like I said, but other days she was tired and slurred and did not make much sense at all. I held on to the days she was lucid, and during those moments, we were able to have a wonderful conversation, and laughed together.

I want *you* to remember that your loved one who has passed or is on the journey now to transition, from this realm to the next, is dying in body, not in soul and in some cases, not in personality either.

The evidence of this I have, and I will discuss in later chapters, but for now, I wish to focus on the journey one makes as a soul.

Once Mum arrived home, I started to read everything and anything I could on life after death, and what actually happens when we die. In fact, now that I really think about it, I started reading about this subject matter the day I learned of her diagnosis. While I always had a fascination with it and had even done a past life regression myself and seen one of my past lives, my interest had piqued.

Mum arrived home late February after my thirty-eighth birthday. All I had on my mind was the fact we had only three weeks left.

I was a wreck emotionally, but I had to stay strong. Never once did I allow her to hear me upset on the phone when we spoke daily. I was upbeat, and now as I reflect on it as I write this, whenever we connected on the phone, I was happy to hear from her. It was almost like for a moment the feeling of dread that I'd lose her was gone. But just for the duration of the conversation. Then when I would hang up, I'd was wrapped up in my own feelings and thoughts, and that's when the grief would return.

All I did to keep strong was read everything I could about the process of dying, and the afterlife. It was almost like I needed to know what journey Mum was on, and where she would go. I researched the process of dying and watched a very interesting documentary on YouTube about near death experiences. I started to learn about how the body shuts down with advanced cancer, so I could anticipate what may be ahead and know when the final days, or even hours, might arrive for Mum, due to the way she appeared.

But what really intrigued me was what happens in that in between stage, as a person crosses over from one life to the next? That's the big question that was unanswered for me.

I learned this is 'the inter-life.' It's the space and time we spend between worlds. People basically return home to the spirit realm, after exiting one life, then prepare for the next.

Mum came home towards the end of February, then developed a blot clot and had to go back to hospital. She spent Mother's Day there, in the UK it's in March, and it was very sad for me. I was still overseas unable to travel. My sisters were caring for her up to this point and discovered the golf-ball size lump on her back. She was rushed back to hospital—again.

Daily, I called, and we spoke. It was all I had, and our conversations meant everything to me. On days where she was too tired to speak, and spent all day sleeping, and was unresponsive to my call, I really lost it emotionally. I worried she was on the decline health wise, or that when I tried to call later that day, or in the morning, she'd no longer be with us.

The last conversation I had with my mum, she was in hospital, and we spoke about food. I am happy to say, even though at this point Mum was not eating anything, or drinking—part of the process of losing the battle to cancer—but during this conversation, she was so upbeat and lucid.

It was the last time I heard my mum's voice. This was about four or five days before she was released from hospital, after they found the clot. During that conversation, our very last one, I told her I was cooking.

Now, Mum liked to cook as much as she loved her gardening, and I love to cook. I thank Mum for the skills I have when it comes to cooking, and my love for good food comes directly from her.

During our final conversation, I was making her

favourite quick meal. So simple, tuna fish and rice. But the tuna fish is seasoned a certain way. There's lots of veggies involved. It's just to die for how Mum made it.

Mine is never as good as hers, but it was close as my son loves it too. If you ask him what he wants to eat, he will blurt out, "Tuna fish and rice." He always makes me laugh.

So, anyway, we had a wonderful conversation about all the foods she liked, and of course, how to make the perfect tuna fish and rice. The conversation left me on a high. And left me happy and hopeful that Mum would be home in a few days. And she was.

The thing is, once Mum arrived home, she slept all day. And that's when there must have been a massive growth with the cancer tumours, especially in her brain. Her speech went away completely. She could no longer speak with me or anyone.

The only contact and connection I had with Mum was gone.

No speech. No memory. I had nothing. She was not even awake for more than an hour each day. Each time I called, she was asleep. I knew she was getting ready to depart and transition from this life to the next, and it was hard.

That week, she finally arrived at her new destination. About four days later, during the night, my mum passed away.

I got off the phone with my sister around nine in the evening. She had been explaining Mum's decline, in health, her inability to move, eat, drink, and so on.

Unable to cope, I had to get off the phone. It was too much for me. But before I did, she took the phone into Mum's room, so I could hear her speak to Mum, and she could try to talk to me.

Mum was out cold, asleep and not really responsive. But what my sister and I thought was sleep, was Mum slipping away, possibly, dipping deeper into a coma.

My sister asked my mum if she wanted water.

A response more like a grunt escaped my mum's lips.

My sister was about to get some damp cotton wool, to squeeze water on her lips because that's the only way Mum could take fluid—she was not able to eat at this point.

Mum mumbled or indicated in a way that my sister intuitively knew that she did not want it, so she left her to sleep.

Once I got off the phone, I remember I just stared at the wall for some time, like I was waiting for it to provide me with some kind of answer to the meaning of life, what was happening, and why my mum had to leave me.

I was not ready. I had never once imagined life without Mum, not once, even as stupid as it sounds, I never did. Like I said, Mum's health was top-notch and she looked more like fifty not seventy.

I started to search for more answers to the meaning of life—and life after death.

That night, I stumbled across a book called, *The Journey of Souls: Case Study of Lives Between Lives*, by Dr. Michael Newton. I was listening blissfully to the audio version, and I felt so much peace, gained so much understanding, and just knew all the evidence he had gathered from people and their experiences was valid.

Now, I've read widely on reincarnation, life after death, contact with the spirit world, mediumship and such. And in my view, this book is probably one of the most impressive to date that I've read. It appeared to me in what some might call divine timing.

Little did I know as I reclined on my sofa, looking up at my ceiling with a feeling of ease soothing my own soul over Mum's journey, she was crossing the water, slipping away. She was transitioning from this realm to the next.

I recalled she heard my sister talking to her, and

she heard our voices, as she did mumble and made a small moan, but she was in between realms, according to what I had learned.

As I gained my peace over Mum's eventual transition, she did just that, she let go and transitioned. Two hours later, after I had gotten off the phone, sometime between nine and eleven p.m., she passed away.

The next morning, my sister told me when she called, she found Mum unresponsive and called the emergency number at 11:02 p.m. the night before.

What I learned from Dr. Newton's book mentioned above is that, when a person passes and leaves his or her body, when she or he is ready to depart Earth and step into the 'tunnel' or 'light' as many of his case studies in his book call it, people are met by a spirit guide.

The journey begins the moment we are greeted. Sometimes, people are also met by loved ones who are waiting, this includes souls who have already passed over. Individuals whom we have connected with in the current life we have left, plus past lives, as well. We then have a meeting with a 'council' of souls who welcome spirits home and 'spirit guides.'

Sometimes if we have left our last life in an extremely traumatic way, not as Mum did in her sleep—say we had an accident or took our own life

—we head to a place to 'rest' and that soul will spend as much time there as they need.

If this is not the case, and we don't need this rest period, we enter the meeting with the council and guides to talk about the life we just left, and the lessons we gave ourselves, before we incarnated into that life.

Then, we move onto a life review. Each significant event of the life left, replayed from birth up to death, we review with the guides. Discussions on the actions taken, and how other people felt depending, on how we treated them—good or bad, come forth. The full impact of those individuals' feelings, come crashing back as the replayed events in life unfold.

We then move into the housing process with a soul group—a group of souls on a similar level of learning and soul development—we all wait together to move onto the staging process, which provides further learning, study, and reviews a soul's individual needs and further learning in order to get ready to move into the next life.

How long we spend in the inter-life, teeters on an individual's needs, how long the review process takes, study and learning requirement, and the connection with other souls we have known, or even boils down to a period of 'rest' if a soul returned home in distress.

However, the concept of time and space people have on Earth, does not exist in the 'other realm' or when one arrives 'home.'

Obviously, I have condensed a six-to-eight-hour audio book full of evidence and case studies down to a paragraph or so. There's a lot more that happens, and Dr. Newton covers so many other topics to answer questions on the inter-life, the afterlife, and he used clear evidence that there was life after death.

Personally, I recommend that you grab yourself a copy of the book or audio. It was such a wonderful read, and even better to listen to in audio. It really soothed my soul, reassured me on my mum's next steps, and it could not have found me it at a better time—two hours before she finally left me, and her soul started its journey to transition home.

So, in a nutshell, yes there is life after death, according to Dr. Newton's years of research and evidence via case studies. And I'm also about to provide a personal account of my own experience that there's life after death.

Our loved ones do communicate in spirit. Sometimes, it's a clear message. So clear, you can't dismiss the possibility that it was them who visited.

5

THE ANCESTOR ALTAR AND THE ANCESTRAL REALM

THE MORNING I received the call from my oldest sister, the one to let me know Mum was no longer with us, I of course, fell apart.

My world crashed.

I had not seen her in person for over a year due to Covid-19. And I never caught on to the fact, she had stopped video calling over the last year. Instead, she had reverted to lots of text messages each day, and an abundance of voice calls.

Guilt ate at me.

How had I missed all the signs?

But when I thought about it, she gave nothing away, didn't reveal that she was ill. The only real change I noticed over the year before she passed, she had really encouraged me to write all the time, everything, anything, and to never stop.

Like I said, I never imagined I'd write a short memoir. I've written nonfiction, of course. Why, I even have a series of books on the craft of writing, and I am a romantic suspense and thriller writer.

But a memoir writer? No way. I never saw that coming.

Mum made me promise to keep going, in fact, she told me, *'if J.K Rowling can, you can too!'*

Meaning one day, I would be a household name author just like J.K Rowling, with my books translated into many languages, with book sales so high, I'd never be able to spend all my royalties.

I laughed as I wrote that section.

I just hope she's right.

But in all honesty, I don't write for the money. I don't think any real or serious writers do. And those who do give up very soon after they start because of low product sells or small reader list—or a lack there of—don't realise success like J.K Rowling's is not something that happens overnight. It might seem as if she was an overnight sensation, but it took time. And not all authors end up down that path. Some never even make to a completed book or manuscript!

That said, I am sure that *this*, writing as a profession, is my job. Now, I find myself in a position to let it be a life-long career for life, I don't intend on stopping. After all, I feel like I owe it to my mum.

It's what she wanted for me.

While we are on the subject of what Mum wanted, and the evidence of the afterlife and spirit communication, I must continue on with my personal account.

The night I proofread this memoir, and before I submitted it to my publisher, I went to seek council from a very trusted psychic medium. I have connected with her many times over the years. So, I told her the story I am about to tell you, about Mum's first Earthly visit.

During the mediumship she did for me, I asked her outright, "Mum is a private person, I don't want to upset her with anything I've written in this memoir, is there anything I need to know before I submit it to my publisher?"

The medium in that session told me Mum was there. She went on to convey Mum had consistently visited me since her passing twelve days ago, and furthermore, she has *'led me by the hand'* with the writing content and full-heartedly approved.

In other words, she loved it.

Now, I must continue to document my experiences with the afterlife, and these works, I hope, will lead others who discover it through a field of flowers and pastures.

In all honesty, I was stunned to hear the woman's words.

'Flowers and Pastures,' now, that was something my mum would say.

The medium told me to, 'follow the 'breadcrumbs' and guidance that she left me. And to pay attention as she would be leaving more of them.

I asked Mum outright at my altar to lead me when needed. This, I will discuss later, along with the message Mum gave the medium for me. The one that confirmed Mum had in fact been in the room with us both.

So, back to the morning Mum passed. Now, Mum was the kind of mother who was practical. She pushed me to charge forward with whatever I want to pursue and go after what I wanted, no matter what.

She always advocated, instructed, and ensured I did what made me happy.

Do not worry about anything or anyone, she often said.

Mum was a practical woman. Some Mums might be overly lovey-dovey or want kids up wrap in cotton wool for full-body protection from the world, nope not Mum. She was a calm and collected individual, even reserved at times, but she was a warrior. And often, she brought out the warrior in me. Not in an aggressive way, but in a survival, self-belief, and achievement kind of way.

She built me up to be confident and know that I can do anything I set my mind to do. Mum helped to shape my identity in a way that no situation, person, place, or thing could ever break my spirit.

For that, Mum, I thank you.

Mum was such a peaceful person. But, now, one thing she did have, and she even passed on to her offspring, was how to be resourceful and not worry about how things will work out.

Focus on the goal—the end result—and it will happen, she used to say.

Often times, I wonder if Mum was such a fierce advocate for me, instructing me to go after my dreams, in all areas of my life, because there were things, she had wished she had done, or wanted to do, and never took that step.

Mum worked hard. She was both mum and dad to me.

She divorced my dad when she was pregnant with me. And the woman had a work ethic that did not allow for things to crumble. If I ever needed anything, Mum provided it, and she taught me to be the same for myself.

If you need something or want something—she had said—*don't worry about how or where it will come from, just keep faith that it will come and keep going after it.*

So, back to the morning I received the emotional call from my sister. Once I placed the phone down, it was seven in the morning.

I remember the day clearly and with vivid detail.

Always up at 5:00 a.m., Monday-Friday, I listened to my affirmations. A podcast with positive news called *Seven Good Minutes*.

Sometimes, I meditate. And when the weather was warm and not too chilly, I sometimes got out of bed and preformed twenty minutes of yoga. By six, I'm behind my laptop writing until nine, then that's when the day, and home-schooling, start.

I love waking up early and seeing the morning sunrise.

I always seem to feel like I achieve so much more in the day if I do. It's how I start my day right. That day in particular, I felt like I needed to wake myself up spiritually, not just physically, I needed to reset my energy for the day. So, on that morning, my whole routine went out the window. I just stayed in bed and listened to Dr. Newton's book, *The Journey of Souls: Case Studies of Lives Between Lives.*

When I eventually got up, and tried to get ready for home-school, I asked my sister to send me a picture of Mum. And I decided that I'd place together Mum's ancestral altar, that day.

This is where my evidence of life after death begins.

What is an ancestor altar you might be asking? It's a dedicated space to one particular ancestor, or your ancestors in general. It could be placed on a table, in a drawer, on a shelf, or a whole room could be dedicated to it.

In the allocated space, one would place candles, a loved one's picture, items they had owned when alive, and things they liked. You could offer the gifts they liked or even just plain water works too.

The altar is a way to 'call' your ancestor. A way to encourage him or her to rest or dwell in your life, and basically a way to honour the individual, his or her life, and encourage your loved one to look out for you—to bring blessing to your life. In return, you give offerings, and never forget.

It's a spiritual practice from many places around the world, especially where my mum was from— across the Caribbean Islands, also in Africa, India, and China.

The setup of an altar may differ from location to location around the world. Also, different cultures contain their own sacred rituals. However, the fundamental use and purpose always remains the same. In the locations around the world mentioned, and within indigenous spiritual beliefs, it's a way to respect, honour, and 'vibrate' the dead, that's the fundamental purpose.

In many indigenous practices and belief systems it was often thought that there was life after death, and that our ancestors can and often do communicate with us. And they can bestow blessing in our lives, if we honour them sincerely. Now, it's a practice outside of mainstream religion, for sure, where life after death has often been shunned.

I should also point out, and at the same time clarify, the western world and many mainstream religions might deem it as 'witchcraft.' Or some kind of devilish practice. It's not.

It's the spiritual practices of the ancestors of those with African descent like myself.

Over the years, these practices passed down from one generation to the next, and they have often been made out to be witchcraft, devil worshipping, and, well, basically trashed or dismissed.

It's upsetting. But has also happened throughout history to pave the way for mainstream religions like Christianity and Catholic religions, which was forced upon the ancestors of those of African descent, during trafficking and slavery.

It stuck, for the most part, and some of the Catholic religion was incorporated into indigenous practices, especially across the Caribbean and on into the southern part of the United States of America.

But that's another story for me to write on a different day—maybe.

The point I'm making here, there's nothing 'bad' about it. I just wanted to clear up this misconception.

6

THE MISEDUCATION OF HOLLYWOOD

VIBRATING THE SPIRIT OF AN ANCESTOR, or deity is common in the Caribbean, Asia, the middle east, and India. It's not for doing evil. It's a form of respect.

To give you just one example of how the western world and especially the mainstream media have really gotten their wires crossed with what many portray as 'devil worship' stuff, one need not look far. Television, motion films, and media have portrayed the African deity called 'Papa Legba' into a program I believe they've titled *An American Horror Story*.

They have him all wrong!

Firstly, Papa Legba in this show has been confused with the Hatian Loa (a God), called Baron Samedi, who is the God of death, along with his wife, Maman Bridgette. Papa Legba and Baron Samedi don't even belong in the same sentence. They are two different pantheons of belief systems: one from Haiti and the other from western Africa.

Anyone of African or Brazillian descent, or even Hatian themselves, which you can class as African descent, would never respect anyone who makes such an error—even if it's for a movie or television show—and take them seriously, thereafter, because they are different, not the same. They are different energies, different Gods, and play very different roles in their respective pathenons of belief systems. But we need them both and worship them as individuals.

Loa (from Haiti) and African spirits or Gods (called Orishas) are totally different, but yet, mainstream media can't even get that right, and what plays out often, disrespects the spiritual systems of those of African descent. Not only that, Baron Samedi is made out to be an 'evil' energy based on how he is portrayed. It appears Baron is some kind of 'hell raiser' instead of the overseer of grief, death, and spirits who have recently returned home.

Papa Legba, also known as Eshu Legba—spelt differently, depending on the island of the Carribean, Brazil, or part of Africa it's used in—or just referred to as 'Pappa' or 'Legba' is a spirit, God, or deity, whatever you wish to refer to him as, governs the 'crossroads.' He is a road opener God, and he is one of the most important.

A Brazillian especially an Afro-Brazillian from the north of the country, will also tell you the same, in Brazil he is so important. Everyone goes to Papa before anyone or anything. He is also a patron of children and is represented as a child sometimes (unlike Baron Samedi). His statue or picture is often placed at the front door of a home to call in opportunities, good luck, remove blocks, and keep the road open in life, bring blessings, and protection.

Often, he's placed even in a child's room for protection from this God. As mentioned, he's a patron for children. And Baron Samedi is not, he's a patron—along with his wife and children—of death, and welcomes the dead home, and he is not evil.

See the difference?

One is for the future and luck in life here on Earth and time and space, and the other is for the after life and protection for when we arrive home in spirit form.

A crossroad is considered the thin veil between Earth, where humans exist, and where the spirit realm resides. The veil remains the thinnest between the hours of three and five in the morning, resulting in a crossroad. Also, a crossroad is the junction of any road where two roads meet, leading to a representation of life and decision making.

If one runs across another, it forms a cross road, similar to a T-junction on a public road. Also, all doorways or front doors are considered crossroads. So, when we have car accidents on the 'road,' a spirit is said to depart quickly (if fatal), as they have exited this incarnation at the crossroads where the veil is the thinnest.

These locations are spiritual places here on Earth to people of African, Brazillian, Carribean, and Puerto Rican descent. Now, I would probably say, for those in the middle East, China, and India too, especially doorways. This is why certain things are placed in doorways, and some things are not. And this is not just a practice for people of African descent, but Chinese and middle Eastern people, too. For example, think of the placement of the 'evil eye' emblem often seen above the door, or as seen above the cash register in the shops of a person of middle eastern descent.

Papa Legba is the first God of one of the 'Seven African Powers,' as mentioned called Orishas—not a Hatian Loa related to the certified religion Vudun, not Voodoo, that's a western misspelling again and often leads to the ideology of 'devil worship.' Now if a person wants any kind of blessing, help, or to speak to any other African deity, one would pray to or call to Papa first, and ask him to 'open the road for communication.'

If a person needed a new start in life and a clear path, one would go and visit Papa at a crossroad, leave him an offering, and ask him nicely for the kind of break or new start the person needed. In turn, he will cut the person some slack and offer help, but only if he agreed with the request.

He is the energy that rests in the 'inter-life' as Dr. Newton called it, *between this realm and the spirit realm, our key communicator and link between God and man. He is one of the most benevolent spirits in African spirituality, and highly respected as the highest God.*

The television showrunners and writers didn't address these points at all. In the television series, when they charactrised Papa Legba with Baron Samedi from Haiti, Baron Samedi is a lot darker in terms of his energy, and that much is true, but not in the way the media had made out. He is not demonic! And Papa Legba simply does not do what Baron Samedi does, so they placed the left shoe on the right foot.

Death is important to many indigenous people and viewed differently than most of the western world see it. We view death as a beautiful event, and we have Gods that 'welcome home' the deceased. We also have Gods associated with death, the after-life, reincarnation, and the inter-life because simply put, we need them, especially based on our belief around death.

I myself know I am protected by or what we would call a daughter of two very powerful female goddesses, you could say, who oversee death from the African pantheons, they welcome the deceased home.

How do I know this?

Because they have shown themselves to me during certain events in my life more than once. And when they did, I could not ignore them, they both gave me a sign.

Now, people say,'I got a sign from God' all the time, well, so did I, but from the female deities. Maybe one day, I'll write about that. But from that single 'sign' I had received, it all made sense, even years before my mum had passed, why I had never been afraid of the dead and found life after death fascinating, and the job of a mortician, or funeral director as we call them in the UK, is one that I could do with no problem and with great joy and respect, even the embalming process—not a problem. Add to all that, how much I love make-up artistry, one would see how I could possibly take pleasure in making sure the dead look their best for their loved ones as they say their final goodbye on the day of the funeral.

As said before, I have a deep respect for the dead. I always have, even before I received my 'sign,' or before my mum's passing, and I always will. I'm not morbid. I just respectful in my own way.

Over the years, my mum had said to me, many times before when she was alive, that *'the dead and spirit world can't harm you, regardless of what people would have you believe about it. It's the living you need to watch out for.'*

My main point here is that the mainstream has got its wires crossed over indigenous belief systems and pantheons of deities. Hollywood has proven this by the way they portrayed their so-called Papa Legba. That is not him.

Lastly, the view of death is so precious and different to indigenous people, and that's why some of us honour our deceased, and celebrate the Mexican holiday 'Day of The Dead' or sometimes called 'Old Souls Day,' annually. Put it this way, if I need support in my life, I am likely to go to the cemetery and place flowers on the first female grave there, as a mark of respect and offering, regardless of whose relative's grave it is. Afterward, I'd go home and pray, or ask one of the female deities who welcome home the dead, or look after my dead ancestors, for support, rather than pray to the God the western world has thrust in my face.

Now, to further explain, the first female grave in any cemetery, no matter what part of the world it is located in, is considered the resting place of these Goddesses, within the pantheon of African deities. No matter who they were in female human form. It's part of the culture of those from African descent, who have not forgotten these sacred practices.

Now, I may have gone totally off topic, but I had to lay a course correction down to help rectify the wrong impression of indigenous people's practices, and the importance and role of Papa Legba in the African pantheon, that mainstream media has showcased incorrectly in both film and television. Also, to give you some context for what you're about to read next.

Just keep in mind, some cultures, not just mine, Asian, Indian, middle Eastern, and Chinese also are deeply respectful of the dead. It's nothing like mainstream religions. And when Old Souls Day or the Day of The Dead rolls around in November, while Mexicans who are close to their cultural practices are celebrating in the street, or cooking large meals for their deceased ancestors, so are many people of African descent, and possibly Chinese, Indian, middle Eastern or Asian people too. It's a happy day, not a day of mourning or 'devil worshiping.'

7

HONOUR THY MOTHER: MY WAY

ONCE I RECEIVED my favourite pictures of Mum, one when she was a picture of health, I printed it off, then started the morning routine, minus the homeschool stuff. After- ward, set off with my son to the supermarket in search of some white pillar candles, and gifts to offer Mum, which I knew she liked while alive.

As I drove to the supermarket, all I could do or think was,

Damn. If only Mum had made it two more months.

It was the 26th of March 2021 by then. I felt angry, funny enough, not with Mum over how she decided to handle things. I could see that she did not want to panic us. I believe that's why she stayed mute that she was dying. I felt sad that all this had happened during the year of the Covid-19 pandemic. So, it's not as if Mum was able to really enjoy herself and make the most of life during her last year.

No. She was confined to her home like the rest of the world, under strict 'stay at home orders,' and fear of her fate if she caught Covid-19 at her age.

I wished I would have had the chance to spend more time with her over that year, but what can I say. I tried to push myself to not dwell as I knew Mum would not have wanted this, she would have wanted me to stay strong, believe, and to know and understand that I would be okay even though she was no longer with me.

My anxious feelings about life started to surface on the drive to store.

That ten-minute ride to the supermarket, sucked every- thing out of me. I was drained emotionally and felt a pain I had never encountered in my lifetime.

Mum, like I had said prior, was my only parent. She was all I had. I could not believe that I was now an orphan.

You may think, *Oh c'mon Kim, that's a bit drastic, orphan really?*

But yes, I do consider myself one, even though I did not lose my mum as a child. She was all I had, a mum and dad all rolled into one beautiful person, since the day I was born, and I loved her dearly.

At the supermarket, I picked up some beautiful white pillar candles to add to the ones I already had at home. I always have them around as I light one each morning and express my gratitude for the day. So, I buy them often. But I wanted new ones, especially for Mum. I also picked up a really nice wine glass, plate, flowers, chocolates, and tea for her.

I returned home filled with grief, my heart heavy. But I put on a brave face and tried to decide where the best place to set up Mum's altar would be.

My hallway contains a peace lily plant, one of my mum's favourite flowers, on a small table with a picture of my grandparents—Mum's parents—above it with candles, incense, and a nice glass of water as an offering. That was the altar I had set up in honour of them.

I considered moving a dresser into that space and placing both my grandparents and Mum on one altar. But an inner voice, my intuition, again, told me to, keep Mum's space private, and to place her where she spent the most time when visiting.

The spare room was the perfect space! No one would see her altar, unless they went in, and I could sit with her there in peace.

So, I unpacked all the purchased items, cleaned

off the dresser, then found a nice scarf Mum had given me, that ironically, was the same shade green as the curtains and bedding. It doubled up nicely as a cloth for her altar.

I then rummaged through the drawers of the dresser. To my surprise, when I opened the bottom drawer, the waft of Mum's scent hit me. She had left some clothes, her handbag, a comb, and knickknacks in the bottom drawer.

Well, I'll be damned!

I could not believe it. I hadn't looked in that drawer for God knows how long.

I could smell her—the actual perfume she had worn.

The tears just fell out of me, and I debated whether I should wash the garment or what to do with them.

Mum had some nice tops, and I was sure I could squeeze into them. Wearing them would be like walking around with her hugging me. So, I decided to wash one that I could wear, folded the rest, then moved them up to the top drawer.

I wanted to preserve as much of her as I could. Also, when it came to preparing an ancestor altar, tradition dictates that you place as many personal items as possible of the deceased person there, so it draws the spirit to dwell there and visit.

A large part of ancestor vibration was not just to honour them as mentioned, but to keep them alive and encourage their presence and blessings as a guide in your life.

I placed Mum's bag and hair comb on top of her altar. Then, I took the time needed to bless and cleanse the candles, glass, and photo frame I had bought for her, then placed the items down on the altar and framed Mum's beautiful picture. As I did this, I felt such a calm and loving energy.

It's like after I smelt her fragrant aroma, gazed at her picture and placed her items on altar—she was alive, present, and I felt so happy and proud of my Caribbean traditions and African descent.

As I filled Mum's vase with water and added one of her favourite flowers—roses, which I managed to find in her favourite colour, peach. I smiled, even through the tears.

Once I had all of Mum's personal belongings arranged with her candles, I set down a representation of all the elements of nature—incense: air, a glass of water; water, crystals that contain high vibrations associated with the third eye chakra; amethyst, clear quartz, and a protective crystal; all of them to represent earth, and a small shot glass of rose wine—to represent spirit, the fifth element.

Now, Mum was not a big drinker. And most of

the time, she drank non-alcoholic wine, would you believe? So, I did buy this version while out, especially to respect her. But if your ancestor liked rum, whisky, or something else, these beverages are perfect offerings and fitting representations of the fifth element 'spirit,' so go for it.

My candles were the representation of fire. I unwrapped my liquor chocolates that I knew Mum liked, and also offered a few on her special plate.

If you're a spiritual person, you may have heard of something called 'ancestor money' or 'joss paper.' In Chinese culture, they offered what they called, 'hell notes' to their ancestors. It's a form of currency printed on paper that they burned. This is because it was said ancestors needed to 'live' in the spirit world, so they give them currency.

In African culture, this was adapted as a form of 'repaying any debts' ancestor's had. People referred to it as 'those who crossed over the middle passage,' referring to our ancestors who were slaves. Whether this be debts for land they owned, or karmatic debts any ancestors had, as well as to offer them currency to 'live' in the spirit realm and pay them for the blessings bestowed on our lives here on Earth.

Also, in African culture, one may go as far as to say that burning and offering ancestor money provides future payment for any offspring's karmatic debts built up over a life, such as my son, his children, and future generations to come.

So, we go down the ancestral line, making offerings and clearing karmatic debts futuristically, as well as back up the line to those who came before us.

It's pretty deep, and respectful if you ask me.

I love what the Chinese do, and I love how my culture has adapted it further to consider the ancestors who passed over. Now, back to my mum. Before I left out that morning, I had printed off a positive quotation and stuck it to some

card, which I placed on the alter too.

Mum was a smoker, and smoke was an excellent offering

to spirits, incense also. So, I purchased a pack a cigarettes and place them down along with my mum's astray that she used when she had stayed with me.

My altar space was done. Mum's personal belongings, a representation of the elements, the offerings of what she liked in human form, a positive quote, and a picture of an African deity, or *Orisha* as we call them. I choose a goddess known as fierce protector, whom from my previous exchanges had let me know she was 'present' in my life as a spiritual parent of mine.

Now, that's another experience of the spirit world to write about all together and at a later date!

I stood back and looked over the beauty of the space I had created for Mum, and I just knew she'd love it. Well, I hoped she would. I did the best with what I could, and she would for sure recognise her belongings from this life—her personal stuff, and all that she liked from flowers, to chocolate, wine preferences, and her smokes.

It felt good, even though I was sad.

I lit Mum's candles and incense and watched the gold flames flicker.

A warmth moved through me. I sat and spoke to her, directly to her picture. We had a full-blown conversation. I won't repeat what was said because that's personal between me and Mum, but basically, I spoke to her as if she were in the room. Told her my hopes and dreams, especially my worries, what I'm doing right now, and asked her most importantly, to 'walk with me and her grandson' in life, to guide us, protect us, and to intervene if she needed to when she knew we're on the wrong path. And most importantly, to never leave us.

I let the candles and incense burn on her altar, told her to enjoy her chocolates, then left the room. My work was done.

I had reached out and openly 'called' her spirit to me with a respectful invitation.

It was her space to dwell in my home. One she would recognise with a picture of herself, all her personal things she used as a woman, and gifts.

For the first time in my life, I had carryout out the first day of a traditional three-day ritual to honour my ancestor.

All I can do now is hope she heard my call.

8

DINNER DATE. MUM, DON'T BE LATE!

THE NEXT DAY, my heart was as heavy as it had been the day before. And the night before, I had continued to listen to *The Journey of The Soul: Case Studies of Lives Between Lives*, by Dr. Michael Newton.

And yes, I felt soothed and hopeful that Mum was now on her journey toward the tunnel, would meet up with her soul group, and rest until she came back again. I wondered if I would ever meet her, and if she would be waiting for me when my time came?

It was a Saturday, and I knew it was the dinner date day of the ritual.

As I rose and started my day, the first thing I did was head into Mum's sacred space, light her candles, bid her good morning, and tell her my plans for the day. Which I remember was to attempt to write the current mystery book I was working on, due to release later in 2021.

A deadline by my publisher loomed. I had to meet it, and I was off track. Well, I felt I was, even though I had time. My goal was to pen it, send it off, and work on the next one—rinse, and then repeat!

I had aspirations to make 2021 a year of productivity. I made a promise to myself, and my mum, I'd keep going moving forward with writing at all costs. I would not waste my talent or opportunity.

It was hard to sit down and allow my creativity to flow. Working became a chore I didn't want to do.

Writing had never felt this way. All I could do was journal and pour out how I was feeling, and what I hoped for. When I was not doing, that I was reclined on the sofa listening to audio books on the afterlife, reincarnation, or reading them. I was also meditating as often as I could to gain some kind of calm.

So, day two, that Saturday morning at Mum's altar, she and I had another conversation. I spoke directly to her. And just as I had done the day before, I left her candles burning all day.

I watched them carefully for safety, of course.

Mum had been gone two days, and it felt so raw to me.

She's really gone.

I could no longer call and check in. Even though in her final days, she was unable to speak to me because her speech had left her with the growth of the cancer on her brain, it was nice to know she was still with us. It sounds selfish, I know. She was with us but was in so much pain. And the drugs that had to be administered, my sister had explained, were so strong and there was a hell-a-lot of them.

Back to the current part of the story. That evening, I prepared a meal for Mum with a lot of love and care. We'd all eat together, that was my plan.

As I said prior, in my last conversation with Mum, when she could still talk, she and I spoke about food. She had expressed her love for simple tuna fish, seasoned well, with veggies and rice. So that's what we were all about to eat.

I made sure I used the right amount of cayenne pepper, chopped the onions nicely, and made sure the rice was nice and fluffy. My avocados were nice and ripe to slice and add on the side of the plate.

As I cooked, I don't want to say I felt happy, as that's really not the way to describe it. But I felt as if I was doing the best I could to maintain a connection with Mum. Most importantly, I was saying goodbye in a way that also meant 'hello.'

It's funny. If you believe in the afterlife, which

clearly you probably do since you're reading this, as I reflect now, saying goodbye to a loved one, as you know, does not really mean a final goodbye.

We here on Earth, living in time and space in this life incarnation, holding on to the hope that the soul is still alive, when a loved one transitions.

From reading Dr. Newton's book and many others on reincarnations, at the time, on this particular Saturday, before I had acquired my own evidence of life after death, I was actually convinced by all I had read, that the soul lives on.

So, once I had prepared the meal, I went to Mum's altar, and then lit her candles and incense. I spoke to her and let her know that I had made dinner, and it was time to eat.

I plated some food for us all, moved my son's small chair and table into the room where Mum's altar was located. I set him up with his plate and juice.

My little son was over the moon we had tuna fish and rice, as I said before, he loved it like Mum did too. He was also very much 'in tune' with what was happening. It was like even though he was just seven years old, he understood something 'special' was happening.

He actually thought it was 'Nana's birthday', with all the candles and chocolates placed on her altar.

To my surprise he never reached for the chocolates. He respectfully stood back, looked over the altar, pointed to the chocolates, spoke to his Nana, and then tucked into his food.

As we all sat and ate, my son was so vocal about Mum.

"Nana's here," he said. "She's going to eat tuna and rice too.'

I just laughed.

But then, during the meal, he asked, "Where is Nana? When can I go see her?" His big, beautiful eyes, full of love, wonderment, and awe, stared at me. "Can we call her?"

"She went to sleep," I told him, and in that moment, my heart broke.

I had never really thought about how to explain Mum's death to my son. He and Mum were close! She spoiled him, like any good grandma does, and they often spoke on the phone.

"Let's call Nana," my son, from a young age, would say at least once a week.

He always wanted to get on the phone. He had a sense of excitement around her. He has the same energy with my oldest sister too.

It's beautiful to see.

So anyway, back to the second night of the

ancestor ritual. The meal came out lovely, and it was a full Moon week.

I'll never forget it. As an astrologer, the Moon phases are important to me.

Through the different phases of the Moon, we can keep tabs on the energy of the Universe, but also, spiritually.

It's important.

Each phase has a particular energy to it, which is good for manifesting, working on goals, and basically working towards being the best version of you.

The full Moon is my favourite time! She's bright, full, strong, and I just love to look at her in the sky. It's funny where I live now, I see each full moon crystal clear in the sky.

Before, I never used to see the moon at all from my window. And on the rare occasion I was out on a full Moon and saw it, it was never as crystal clear as it now appears in my new home.

So, as we sat and ate, I left the curtains open, so we could bask in the beautiful energy of the full moon. Once we had consumed our meal, I cleared the space and once alone, I prayed openly to the universe for Mum's well-being on the other side, and for my own wealth, health, abundance and fortune that I was due, for the universe to bless me with it.

I openly invited Mum again into to my life and asked her to never leave me. I also thanked her for being the best mum I knew she could be. And I expressed my gratitude for her eternal love and protection.

Before I left the room, I checked the burning candles, then lit some fresh jasmine incense. A scent I know Mum loved.

She had grown the plant in her garden, and she planted it strategically next to where she sat on her bench, as well as by the back door. Mum always said it was so the scent could blow into the house.

I shed one final tear, said good night to Mum, then reached for another book on the afterlife.

My Saturday night was spent in reflection, reading, and contemplating the afterlife. Before bed, I went back into the room and kissed Mum's photo, then went to sleep.

9

MESSAGES FROM BEYOND THE GAVE

The next morning, the 28th of March 2021, was day three of my ancestor ritual to honour Mum.

It was a bright and sunny morning, and I had a peaceful sleep. Once up, I opened the back door, made coffee, lit my usual candle for myself and expressed gratitude for the day, and life.

My son came bounding into the kitchen, ran outside the open door in his pajamas to play, and I just laughed.

While he played outside, I went to Mum's altar, lit her candle, a jasmine incense, and said good morning.

I had another conversation with her. And I promised her that today, I would write.

Well, at least, I would try.

I openly spoke directly to her about what a nice day it would be.

The sun was out, and it felt like a wonderful spring morning. A time of year Mum loved—her favourite season.

She had always said it was because that's when her garden came to life. The plants and flowers started to bloom. And it was not too hot, nor to cold.

Even though my mum was born in the Caribbean, the heat was not something she loved. I blame that on most of her life spent in the United Kingdom, where summer is about two weeks of twenty-degree heat, if we're lucky.

She became used to this rather than the thirty plus heat of the island she was born on.

Me personally, I love spring, yes, but give me summer—a Caribbean summer any day! I love it and we'd often debate it.

She felt the heat in London was too overbearing due to the pollution, and lack of breeze with all the high rise buildings. There was no sea or enough open space to welcome in a breeze. She had a point, as every time I have been to a hot location, be it summer in Las Vegas, Jamaica, Portugal, Spain, or the south of France in the peak season, the heat was hotter, but it did not feel as uncomfortable, compared to London.

So on that beautiful Sunday, I stood by Mum's altar and connected with her again, and told her to have a nice day wherever she was.

Even though I was aware she was no longer living in time and space like I was. I left her candles and incense burning, then I headed back to make breakfast and coffee.

Within an hour maximum of me leaving the room, my son approached me.

"Can I go into the paddling pool," my son asked so sweetly. "Please?"

"Sure," I said. "Why not. It's a lovely day."

I headed back into the room where Mum's altar was, as the pump for the paddling pool was stored in the cupboard there. And to my surprise, when I entered to room, the window by her altar was wide open.

In shock, I stood motionless for about ten-seconds, looking around the room, and at the window. I was overwhelmed with the sight.

Now, to have a firm understanding of the situation at hand. To open *that* particular window, you have to turn the handle 180 degrees to the right, then pull it towards you, so the rods will release, and it can open.

My friend, let me tell you something, that window had been securely locked.

It hadn't been opened at all, before or after Mum's passing during 2021.

I had not opened it or needed to.

Everyone was outside, and to be honest, I don't open that window ever because it's located at the front of the house. I worry my son will approach it and topple out. So, in a nutshell, I'm too scared to ever open it, especially when not in the room.

It's a huge window, and my son, always drawn to that room, knows the area as 'Nanny's room.' He randomly goes in there and jumps on the bed and plays with his cars and all sorts of other toys—simply because 'it's Nanny's room,' so, for safety reasons, I don't run the risk of opening it—ever.

I glanced over at Mum's altar.

The candle and incense were still burning.

I could not work out why it was. I mean, the window was wide open and the wind blowing.

Why didn't the wind blow it out? But that was not the key question for me to ask, no.

My logical brain kicked in, and I started to look at the window closely, even inspected the lock.

Nothing was out of place.

I closed it, locked it, then opened it again, paying close attention to the level of detail and effort needed to open it up.

A visitor came calling.

Mum had made it clear to me, she had paid a visit. She was fully aware of the ancestor ritual I had done, seen her altar space, and she clearly heard my call. The opened window was the confirmation, and it was a direct communication from the other side.

Now, at this point, I would like to and fast forward, slightly.

The night I proofread this manuscript, before I sent it to my publisher, you might now recall me mentioning, at the start of this story, how I connected with a trusted psychic medium I've worked with before.

Well, I wanted to check I had not offended Mum with anything I had written, and see if Mum had a message for me, after all, she had visited me three days after her death.

The medium told me, "Your Mum has been leading you by the hand to write, and for you to follow her, she's very pleased." She drew in a breath then continued, "The work was discovered, and she loved it."

In addition, the medium gave me a very clear message before she sent me on my way.

"Your Mum loves the altar. It's sacred though. And she would love to have more tea with you," she said in a cheerful way, as if Mum was laughing about it.

My friend I was in tears, and my mouth hit the floor.

Yes! I had given my mum tea as a personal offering twice in the twelve days before I connected with the medium. In fact, I had given her normal tea, and herbal. On some days, I did not give her tea. But I drank a cup of tea myself and spoke to her at the altar.

I also asked that my sister mail me one of Mum's mugs that she used to drink her tea from, so I could place it on her altar. It arrived the same day I went to the spiritual medium.

What the medium told me next, further proved to me, there was life after death, and spiritual mediums—genuine ones can connect a person to a loved one.

"Oh, your Mum really likes the roses, and the rose tea."

Now, if you remember, in an earlier chapter, I told you that on top of Mum's altar, I had placed one of her favourite flowers—roses, and in her favourite colour, peach.

Well, all this communication came through to me the night before I was due to submit this memoir to my publisher.

I had to ensure Mum was not upset with my

work. So, let me regress back to the day I actually walked into the room and found the window open.

Once I discovered it, I ran out of the room to get my phone, and then I did something, I recorded a video of me opening and closing the window. I wanted to show my older sister the effort needed, and that this was no mistake.

Mum had been in the room, or, at least, her spirit and soul had. I was sure of it.

I saved the video, then I did something that one in my ancestral spiritual belief system must never do because it's totally forbidden.

I documented the room through recording.

Now, let me explain something in greater detail.

An ancestor altar is sacred. You never, and I do mean never, if you want to remain true to tradition, share it with videos, pictures, or willingly let others see it.

If a person visits your home and notices it, or sees it, or even admires it, that's fine and normal. But you don't go out of your way to show an ancestor's altar to anyone.

Now, I'm fully aware of this. Folklore states it's because spirits clearly don't like it. It's their personal space that you honour and communicate with them through.

Well, the same goes for deity altars if you feel connected to a God of your choice. But me being me, I reasoned that if I took a video of Mum's altar to show how close it was to the window, and the strangeness over the open window, and candle still burning in the wind, and then share it only with my sister, I would not be doing anything wrong.

I rationalised it would be okay because it was for my sister—Mum's eldest daughter, so there was no way Mum would be pissed, or against it, right?

So, I did just that. I recorded a new video speaking to my sister directly.

"I know I'm not meant to do this, but it's you," I said to my sister. "Mum won't be upset."

I showed her how close the altar was to the widow, then decided to add to the video to the first one I made, showing how to open the window. And, in truth, I wanted to share with my sister, Mum's beautiful space.

It was totally innocent—even if it was against the 'rules.' *It should be fine, right?*

I managed to attach the first video that was probably about thirty-seconds or so to a WhatsApp message. This was the video showing my sister what's involved in opening the window. The second video contained Mum's altar along with my clear confession of knowing that I should *not* share the video. But it would not attach.

In fact, it went blank, the screen froze, then crashed.

In frustration, I went back to the gallery on my phone where the videos were saved.

My friend it was gone! Gone, gone, gone, gone like a thief in the night, gone! Where the hell was it? Where did it go?

I had no evidence of the video I recorded, and I still don't to this very day. It's as if I never even recorded it, but I know I did.

I recorded it! So, what can I say?

Well, we all know spirits communicate and mess with electricity, water, and technology. Mum no doubt snatched that video off my phone.

I imagine this was to one, reprimand me and let me know that it's not *okay* to ever share her space with another person like that—even my sister, her eldest daughter.

And I believe the action was preformed to give me further confirmation that she was there, she had not left me.

My mum opened the window and deleted my files.

I was gob-smacked, and all I could do was smile, and shed tears of joy.

Let's fast forward to when I connected with the spiritual medium thirteen days later, the actual day I physically wrote this piece. I wanted to know if Mum had, in fact, visited me, opened the window, and then removed all of my recordings of her altar?

Now, after the whoopsie I did by recording the altar, I did not want to upset her again. I don't think I did, she just cleared off my video from my phone to reinforce 'the rules,' and to remind me to remain respectful to our traditions.

Even if it's my sister, we both wish to share the altars we respectfully erected in Mum's honour in our respective homes, we learned, one does not cross the line and show Mum's space to anyone.

"She said it's sacred," the medium said to me when we last spoke.

So, yes, Mum removed the recording. But now, at least, I know she is not upset with me.

So back to the day of the open window, three days after Mum had passed.

Once the recording vanished from my phone, and I had opened and closed the window about fifty times, checking it over and over again, I did not want to leave the room.

I did not feel a 'presence' of her there at all. The energy in the room felt like normal. You see, I am very sensitive to energy, and Mum never showed herself to me in any form. But she showed me that she was present and had very much found her sacred space, but she was not prepared to let it be shared.

Mum, I'm sorry. I apologised from the bottom of my heart, of course. I gave an offering of tea to her to say and express my sorrow.

As I write this now and reflect back, it's so touching for me. If you remember, I've confirmed that the medium told me, 'Mum wishes she could have more tea with you.' Hold on to that thought.

The day of the open window and deleted files, which was the third day after her passing, was one of the days I offered tea to Mum. It was an apology for the recorded altar I almost shared with my oldest sister, if my mum had not stopped me.

Now, during my meeting with the medium, she passed on Mum's message and desire to have more tea with me, around twelve-thirteen days after the open window, deleted files, and the offering of tea as an apology had all happened.

So, this is yet more confirmation of Mum being present on both occasions. First, on the day of the open window and the recording, which she deleted off my phone, and then secondly, during the mediumship session almost two weeks later.

After that clear visitation and communication from Mum, I had no further communication that week.

My three-day ritual had not been completed, at

least, as far as I was concerned, and it was only late morning. I hadn't done the final day's offering and prayer. In fact, the tea was an apology, not an offering from the heart.

But that said, the day passed well. I enjoyed spending time outside in the sunshine with my son, and I devoured yet more reading and research into life after death, and spirit communication.

Spirits visit their loved ones shortly after they passed over, well, from what I have read anyway, *they do it before they finally move toward the 'tunnel' or 'light' and head back home.*

I rest in the knowledge that Mum has possibly gone over.

Some content I've read, say that on the day of the funeral, an ancestor returns—some do, anyway.

Mum's body has not been laid to rest yet. The Covid-19 pandemic has resulted in a funeral waiting list, would you believe, with the funeral directors.

On the same day Mum visited me and found her altar space to dwell in my life, I decided to give offerings and connect with Mum at her altar for seven days, not three.

So, I did, but I had no further visits.

But I did notice that I slept well each night, even if I was up until four in the morning thinking, crying, and missing Mum.

When I stopped on the seventh day with her offerings, which will now be weekly on a certain day, I did not stop saying good morning or good night to her.

And every morning, I light Mum's candles on her altar and talk to her.

One morning, I woke up so filled will grief, it was a hard day—some days remain harder than others. But on this day of sadness, when I woke, I stayed in Mum's room all day. I just looked out the window, daydreaming, and shed tears. I spoke to her as well.

That day, as I sat there by her altar, filled with grief, a story plot—featuring an open window as part of the mystery—came to me.

This I know is Mum at work, I was sure of it, *and it's more communication from beyond the grave.*

But I did not have confirmation of this until I met with the medium on that one day. Her words still linger in my mind, even now.

"Mum is leading you by the hand with writing," she said. "Follow the guidance and 'bread crumb trail' she leaves you."

For some time, I had been thinking of what story I should add next to my Unsolved Mysteries series that showcases stories from around the world.

I wanted to head to a Caribbean Island and cook up a who-dun-it story there.

No one knew this, only me.

Maybe I was wrong all along, and Mum knew and said, "Here, take this and run with it."

I had a writer's intuitive feeling that the concept would flesh out to be more of a short-story, or novella rather than a full novel.

Mind you, I say that all the time, and then my work in progress ends up a lot longer. My editor can confirm that!

So, I wiped my tears and contacted my publisher to see if they were still seeking short stories from their signed authors. After all, I now had a fictional short story to pen. I also explained how the story had come to me.

Oddly enough, a few months back, I was told about the call for submissions, but never had anything at the time to write—not even an inkling of a concept.

I sent out the enquiry, and a response came back that they were, in fact, actually seeking non-fiction works, and they encouraged me to share my life after death experience this way.

Well, I gave it all of thirty-seconds of thought, if that, and decided, *yep this would be more meaningful as a memoir.*

For someone like you, who is just like me—seeking the truth and evidence of life after death. As well as some comfort. Or for someone who may need reassurance, a sign of how they can connect with their loved ones and feel that an ancestor altar may just be the way, I typed this for you.

I also felt at the time, and still do, that using my direct experience with Mum's communication from beyond the grave, would be an excellent tribute to her and a way to show her that, *yes, I am still writing!*

So, I will not give up, even through my grief. Lastly for me, during the writing process of this memoir, the words just flowed with ease and it has felt like additional healing, and step forward in this life incarnation for me without my beloved Mum.

She's still here, in spirit if not in body, and your love one is too, or will be if they have not passed over yet.

Death isn't the end, my friend. It's only another page. And what I have shared with you, within these pages, is that there is clearly life after death. You only need to look for the signs.

The same day I toyed with writing this short memoir, I had started to feel a presence in the kitchen. I don't know how to explain it, or if you've ever felt anything akin to it before. But every time I walked into the room, the energy of the area just magnified and felt different.

I felt, well, not like I was being watched in a negative way, just as if I was not alone. Especially when I stood by the cooker to cook, which to the right-hand side is where Mum stood when she visited to keep warm. *The radiator is there.* It's a large one, she had stood there to sip her tea.

Imagine that, I just knew it was her. From what I've read in a number of books, and especially in Michael Newton's body of work, souls are able to travel between our realm and theirs once they have crossed over. And they move at the speed of a thought.

Imagine that!

So, once our loved ones cross over, they can be back as soon as we think of them. Or even if we don't, they can appear in our space and energy if they wish to just as quick as a thought enters in one's mind.

The week that I got the go ahead to write this and submit my manuscript, Mum was very present in the kitchen on that Monday, watching over me. I got the go ahead on Tuesday. And on that day, she was very present in the kitchen—nowhere else in the house—just the kitchen.

Like I said, Mum was a good cook and she liked to prepare meals too.

Rest assured, your loved one is always nearby.

Even if they don't show themselves to you in a visual image, pay attention to the energy in your home, or when you feel a sudden change of energy around you. Those of us who are more sensitive to energy, and emotionally intelligent—empathic—are at an advantage to notice it.

Stay open to the possibilities of life after death.

10

MOVE FORWARD. NEVER FORGET

Mum has only been gone thirteen days as I write this section, and a lot has happened as you can see. I am now fully certain that there's life after death. I don't doubt it, and I don't want you to either. If you feel drawn to make your own ancestor altar, I encourage you to do so. You can find all you need below:

—A picture of your ancestor.

—A white candle for purity and protection. I would recommend a large pillar one.

—A glass of water.

—An offering, of what they liked when they were alive.

These are the bear minimum. I added things to represent the elements, personal belongings of Mum's, an image of a protective deity, incense, flowers, a pack of cigarettes, a positive quote, and ancestor money. You may add these and if you're religious, even some Psalms from the bible of your choice would do.

These are additional things highly recommended and used in many cultures who appreciate ancestor altars, but as a bare minimum, the four things above are fine. Don't stretch beyond your budget.

My biggest bit of advice, create a space that represents the person at his or her core—who the individual was and what they liked. This is so the person recognise him-or-herself there.

Give offerings to your ancestor often, on a schedule that suits you, or even do the three-day ritual that I did to start and extend it to seven as I did with offerings each day if you so wish.

I would say, don't worry if you don't get any clear communication from them like I did. Each soul that has passed over acts differently, and Mum had just passed, so calling her in was probably slightly easier for me since she had just left her body within in less than twenty-four hours before I put up her altar.

The main thing is, if you have done it, your loved one will recognise it. And it's for you as much as for that someone special. It's a way for you to move forward but never forget. Whenever you wish to talk or connect with an ancestor, just go to the altar.

I will never be in a space where I am ready to let Mum go, she means too much to me.

Her death was so untimely, shocking, and heartbreaking, not just because she never told us, but because Mum was fit and healthy and had so much vitality in her. And like I said, I never prepared myself for having to live without Mum, purely because I just took this thing called life for granted, I guess. Not in a negative way.

When someone says to you, "Life is short!"

Listen and absorb the words, I must say because Mum's death has shown me how short life can be.

The best thing to do, enjoy this life incarnation we are all in and make the most of it.

That's what I intend to do, for me, and for Mum, as I know that's exactly what she would want.

She wouldn't want me to be sad for too long, lose my way, drop off of my goals, dreams, and aspirations. Most importantly, I know she'd be angry if I stopped writing for a long period of time. Therefore, I have no choice but to keep going if I want my mum to truly rest in peace.

Take each day as it comes, especially if your loved one has just passed.

There will be good days, where you get through, and then there's no tears or heartache. There will also be days like the one when I started to write this memoir, when you get out of bed and have no motivation, drive, wish, or desire to do anything but sit by your ancestor's picture and cry in disbelief.

On those days, go to the altar, light your candles and speak from the heart. Be gentle on yourself and think about how you will ensure that the next day will be a better day, and you will move forward slowly, but never forget them.

I really hope you found some comfort in my real-life experience. I wish you lots of love, light, and healing on your journey.

A NOTE FROM THE AUTHOR

A QUICK NOTE ABOUT THE 'NONBELIEVERS' that you'll come across as you read more about life after death, or even have your own experience. I had a deeply religious family member try to discourage me from believing that Mum's spirit was present in the room she last slept in, that she could never have opened the window which requires a 180 degree turn of the handle. But everyone in the house was outside and I had just spoken with Mum in the room at her altar less than an hour before.

"There's no way Mum's spirit interacted with your technology and deleted the video of her private ancestor's s altar from your phone, or before your very eyes," this person went on to say.

This family member even went as far as to tell me that, the spiritual medium could not interact with Mum's spirit, because 'Mum's with God and the medium works with demons.'

For a moment, I felt heartbroken this person could be so dismissive more than anything else. But my faith did not waiver in life after death and this is because, no matter how much those who are deeply religious wish to stamp over the idea that there's no life after death and the spirit 'rests with God or hell', there's more evidence out there to prove otherwise.

Just look at the esoteric book market. It's flooded with near death experiences, life after death stories, reincarnation experiences, or past life regression memories. People have been to the other side and back generation after generation, there's no doubt. Are they all liars, cheaters, and out to make a quick buck? Doubt it.

Now, I'm not out to bash any religious individuals because a person's individual belief is his or hers alone. The purpose of this body of work is to explore the belief there's life after death because there's too much evidence to suggest otherwise, but by now, you know how I feel about mainstream religion personally. While spiritual, I don't subscribe to mainstream views and don't fault those that do. As I stated before one's belief is a personal choice.

My main message here, forget what anyone else says, and keep an open mind. I want you to stand firm in your belief or curiosity into the possibility of life after death, because it's not a 'possibility' it's a reality. And I feel so happy that I'm someone who can contribute personal written evidence to the esoteric book market, so I can help satisfy those who seek the truth.

My experience is my own. My encounter is personal. My account is authentic.

You will come up against opposition, people will try, but only if you allow them, to make you feel crazy.

Don't allow it. Don't entertain it. Don't feel pressured to look the other way.

If you connect with the spirit of a loved one, the evidence is more likely to support the argument that it was them, rather than it wasn't them who made contact. If it happens, and you feel that connection, don't ever question it—it happened.

Stay open. Listen to the messages. Look for signs. Keep your love for them alive in any way you wish.

Not a day will pass by without me lighting the candle on my mum's altar and bidding her good morning. I will talk to her about life when I feel like it, or leave her favourite chocolates, and have tea with her—just as she asked me to drink tea via the psychic medium.

And while I'm on the subject of mediums, did you

know spirits have a way of placing things in alignment? Or, at least, I think so.

For those wondering how it's possible for a person, in this case a medium, to connect with an ancestor? Let's use my mum as an example. She more than likely engineered a plan for me to go to the medium. I feel the 'push' I felt to reach out to the medium came from mine and Mum's need to reconnect. As mentioned, I have connected with that lady before, a while back actually, and Mum on the other side with her new perspective of me, knew that, and knew if I'd trust any spiritual medium, it would be that lady.

The spirit guides of mediums are those individuals who pass on the message from our loved ones to the medium. It's like a triangle, so to speak. The guide of a medium only allows certain spirits to interact with their human, our loved one stands on one side of them, the guide on the other. And a loved one gives the message, the spirit guide passes it on in the best way possible for the medium to understand, depending on his or her gift.

So, my medium told me Mum had passed on the image of a kettle, and cup, and she heard, *'she'd like to have more tea with you and laughed'.*

Mum passed on the image of roses, her favourite flowers. And the flowers, I placed on her altar with full knowledge that my mum would love them. My medium is clairvoyant and clairaudient, meaning she receives her messages by both hearing and seeing, that's her connection with her guide.

I know this only because years ago, I read about how spirit communication works, and it's always been the same, consistent message from mediums. Mediums are also people who have made agreements with their spirit guides before they incarnated into this life, to be a portal between both worlds! It's fascinating, but I'm going off topic.

However, a word of advice, when it comes to mediums, be sure to check their reviews from other customers. Only go to well-reviewed websites to seek them, and don't give them too much information. Instead, listen to what they have to say, and see if their message resonates with you.

Sadly, there are fake mediums out there, but there are also genuine, spiritually gifted people who walk this earth and serve a purpose as a portal between us, here on Earth, and the other realm. We all have spirit guides. It's just some people are more sensitive and can hear them clearer and are mediums.

Do your research on a potential medium. Work with the individual, seeking basic guidance at first, then if you feel comfortable, and the person is an actual medium—not just psychic as there's a difference—see if anyone you love has a message from beyond the grave. And if you have a story to tell, I encourage you to tell it, write it, or paint it. Record it in some form or fashion or find someone with the skills to help you.

Keep believing. Keep seeking the truth. Keep an open mind.

Love,
 Kim

ABOUT THE AUTHOR

Kim Knight was born in 1983 and from London in the UK. She's a mother to a beautiful little boy, an award winning romantic suspense and thriller author, and the #1 Best-Selling Author of 365 Days of Writing Prompts for Romance Writers, also The Art of Self-Editing for Writers. She's also a best-selling author of an Unsolved Mysteries Series. As a reader she's head over heels in love with romance, historical fiction, crime fiction, African-American, suspense and thriller genre books. As a writer, Kim enjoys creating steamy stories with a diverse and multi-cultural line up, within the romance, romantic suspense and general thriller and crime genres.

Connect with me on social media here

- Bookbub - Follow me here: www.bookbub/kimknight
- Facebook - Give my page a like and follow me here: @kimknightauthoruk
- Twitter - Tweet at me @kimknightauthor

- Author site - Catch up with all my day to day shenanigans and other featured authors here: www.kimknightauthor.com

SNEAK PEEK OF THE NOTE

Everyone has a motive for murder when there's money on the table. But whose story is more plausible?

In seventy-two hours, Detectives Idris Dunne and Josh McDonald close in on an unsolved murder case with the help of mysterious notes.

One of London's wealthy entrepreneurs was diagnosed with cancer, and became estranged from his wife of thirty years Manisha. Unknown to her, his mistress Chelsea Jackson was slowly sinking her claws into her husband. But that's not all his mistress was up to. Unexpectedly Tony's mutilated body is found dumped in a park. Everyone has a motive especially when money is on the table, and his wife Manisha, and their adult children were cut out of his will and replaced by his mistress Chelsea.

Was this an act of kindness from Tony, toward his carer and mistress? Or was there foul play and pressure to change his will by Chelsea? What about his murderer? The case was left unsolved, with lack of evidence.

Mystery notes are sent by an anonymous tip off, Detective Dunne and McDonald re-investigate and piece together the mystery surrounding the entrepreneur's death, and what led him to change his Last Will in Testament. The question is, from all suspects whose story is more plausible?

1

SLEEPING DOGS, WAKE

DETECTIVE DUNNE

Early Monday morning, Detective Idris Dunne ran a hand over his stubble, adjusted his chair, and watched the computer screen in anticipation. After several seconds, he paused the homemade video tape. He glanced at the plain brown envelope it had come in—left in his mail slot overnight.

He grinned, then shook his head.

Snatching up the phone, he hit redial, then waited impatiently for an answer.

"Yeah," his partner's voice boomed down the line.

"McDonald, you need to get in here and take a look at this." Dunne moved his eyes back over to the screen.

"What's up? Sounds serious."

"It is. That case we thought was closed—looks like there's more to it." Dunne leaned forward in his chair and narrowed his eyes at the screen. He noted the date stamp on the video.

"Which one?"

"The old guy with the stab wounds, missing both eyes, he was found on the common. He left all his money to the young girl. You must remember?"

A beat of silence fell over the line. "Ah, yeah, how could I ever forget." McDonald chuckled. "The whole family contested the hell out of his will, that's him, right?"

"That's the one. Get in here, something's come up."

Dunne dropped the phone on the receiver, then sat upright in his chair. He glanced at his Rolex. The dial showed 9.30 a.m., and he had work to do.

"This is some bullshit." He rubbed his tired, bloodshot eyes. "Already, this day smells and feels like some shit's heading my way."

He glanced around his office, crammed with filing cabinets, paperwork, endless coffee mugs, and boxes of energy snack cereal bars.

With gloved hands, he picked up the brown envelope, slid out a piece of paper from inside, then sat back in his chair. He frowned, cursed again, and raised his eyes to the ceiling in disbelief. Glancing back at the note on his desk, he took in the carefully placed letter cuttings from a newspaper. The new evidence brought more questions to mind than it answered.

> YOU NEED TO CHECK THIS GIRL OUT, SHE IS NOT INNOCENT, SHE WAS ONLY AFTER HIS MONEY. HE WAS SET UP!!

A quick inspection of the envelope didn't shine any new information on the case—no return address, no time or location to indicate where it was sent from stamp, nothing. And if he were a gambling man, he'd bet a year's salary, he wouldn't find prints, either.

Dunne scoffed, dropped the note on his desk, then removed his gloves. As one of London Metropolitan Police's top detectives, he had his fair share of hate mail. But this was different.

"Damn. We closed this case," he protested to no one in particular, "it was a family feud, bitterness over a dead man's last Will in Testament."

Rising, he got up from behind his desk and made his way over to the window in his office that overlooked the financial heart of London. Outside, the grey sky was about to cave in and give way to a downpour. The morning's hustle and bustle played out below him.

City workers moved back and forth across his vision, scurrying around on the street below.

A quick glance behind him, and his gaze locked on the note. He contemplated the firm push the note had given him to check out the case again. With his back to the view of London, he faced the filing cabinet filled with cases he thought he had closed.

"What did I miss?"

He questioned, as if in doubt over his own investigative skills, which pissed him off even more.

Nah, I don't miss a beat, never, been doin' this too long, he mused. But this ain't right.

He made his way over to the cabinet and thumbed through the dusty, thick, paper files. Once he found what he was looking for, he shook his head, dug out the bulky envelope, and then approached his desk, dropping it on the surface.

His fingers latched onto the fabric covering his thighs, and he hitched the legs of his smart trousers up, then took a seat.

"The wife"—he sighed—"always suspect number one."

He pulled out the transcripts of the interviews he

and McDonald had carried out with Manisha Patel, the dead man's estranged wife. His eyes roamed over dates, times, locations, and her alibi for the twenty-four hours before Tony Patel was found dead.

"Airtight." He tapped the page that confirmed her alibi that night. "It checked out."

Hands clasped in a prayer position, he inhaled deeply. After a beat, he picked up the remote control, then rewound the tape to the start.

The door creaked open, and McDonald entered, closing the door behind him.

"Where's the fire?"

McDonald's six-foot-two frame leaned against the door, arms folded across his muscular chest.

Without a word, Dunne nodded to the chair next to his desk.

McDonald strode over to the worn, leather chair, then sat.

Speechless, Dunne slid on his gloves, then held up the note to his partner.

Without touching it, McDonald's eyes trailed back and forth, reading the contents of the page. The corners of his lips curled, and his ice blue eyes met Dunne's gaze.

"What's this?" McDonald's cocked eyebrow protruded in Dunne's direction.

Dunne shook his head, he hit play, and then let the video speak for itself.

On screen, were a couple sat in a car, sharing an intimate moment—fogging the windows with the increased heat of their combined bodies. To an outsider, it appeared as if they were doing no harm.

"You've got to be kidding me," McDonald's voice boomed around the small office. "She was having an affair?"

He watched the video recording eagle-eyed. The girlfriend, and heir to a substantial estate, romped around in the back of a car with an unknown man.

"Yep, looks like it. Maybe the family were right after all," Dunne dryly responded, then pulled off his gloves and paused the tape.

"What was her name?"

"Chelsea Jackson," replied Dunne.

"That's right." McDonald leaned his head to one side. "Is this really enough to open up a can of worms?"

He had worked with Dunne long enough to read his mind—or damn near close. He knew where his partner was headed with this line of talk already.

"Think about it, this could've been after he died."

Dunne shook his head. "Nope, look at the date stamp on the video."

McDonald narrowed his eyes at the screen and

let out a low whistle. "The same month his body turned up."

"Bingo, exactly. I checked over the records. It was three days before to be exact."

"Jesus." McDonald ran a hand over his face. "We got bigger fish to fry right now."

"Tell me about it. But it's worth looking into." Dunne tapped the paused screen, "Someone went out of their way to get this tape and note to me."

McDonald met Dunne's eyes and locked gazes with him. "What do you mean?"

"Exactly that," Dunne snorted. "I walked in this morning, and Shelly told me it was in my mailbox with the rest of the incoming mail. Someone mailed it."

"Hmm, whoever it was doesn't want you to know who they are."

McDonald reached inside a desk drawer, extracted a pair of gloves, then picked up the note. He looked over it in silence, then placed it together with the envelope.

"Right. That's what I figured too."

Dunne sighed, then dragged a hand through his beard. He got up and went over to the coffee machine, that looked like a museum relic, in the corner of the room.

"This damn thing needs replacing." He fiddled around with the buttons.

The machine hiccupped to life and started to warm the liquid inside.

"First thing's first," he called over his shoulder, "the guy, what was his name . . . Patel, Tony Patel?"

"That's it, yeah."

"Eyes gauged out, stab wounds to the face, neck, and chest, dumped on the common, no weapons found, no suspects nailed, nothing—a complete dead end."

He recalled the images of the case, reassigning them to current memory.

From the middle shelf of the cabinet, he pulled out two mugs with deep coffee stains ingrained in the ceramic. No matter how much he scrubbed them, they never disappeared.

Dunne pinched his face up. Ignoring the rings, he poured the hot, dark liquid into the cups.

"Right, exactly. It's been months, so why now? That's what I don't understand." McDonald turned his attention to the paused video. "Why has this person taken so long to hand this evidence over?"

Dunne slowly placed the coffee mug on the corner of the counter, glanced over his shoulder at McDonald and the note on his desk.

"That's what we need to find out." He focused on

the second empty mug, void of the bitter-tasting, department cheap coffee he had grown to appreciate.

Glancing at the half empty container in the cabinet, containing the emergency supply he used only when he ran out of his own special blend, he let out a heavy sigh. It would have to do for now.

McDonald got to his feet and picked up the mystery note. "All right, let's pay a visit to his girlfriend, that's if she's not skipped the country by now."

Dunne chuckled. "Hmmm, could you blame her? I'd swap London's pollution for a beach any day."

"Yeah, right." McDonald let out a deep laugh. "You're chained to the shackles of this place just like me. You love it. Don't lie."

Dunne joined in with his partner's laughter. "Whatever, man."

2

MONEY TALKS

Lance

Lance glanced from under the bonnet of the old Ford he was working on. Through the engine's smoke fumes, he noticed a shadow and sighed. "What now?"

He moved from under the hood of the car, turned around, and reached for the dirty rag on the ground, then wiped his grease-stained hands.

"Lance, it's been a while," a scratchy voice, with tell-tale signs it belonged to a heavy smoker, crept up from behind. "Where ya been hidin'?"

Lance rolled his eyes and gritted his teeth.

"All right, John, yeah . . . I've just, well, been a bit busy, that's all."

He lied and wrapped the dirty rag around his fingers. His anxiety shot through the smoke-stained tin roof of the crammed garage he owned.

John let out a low whistle and took slow steps towards him from the entrance of the garage.

Lance eyed him with suspicion. A visit from the local loan shark always brought trouble along for the ride.

"Busy?" John walked around the side of the car, so he was toe-to-toe with Lance.

Of similar height, John looked him dead in the eye, then lowered his voice. "You must have my money then, aye?"

Lance stepped back and tripped over the toolbox on the floor. The screwdrivers flew out the box and scattered along the grease-spotted floor.

"Well . . . I, no. John, not yet just give—"

"No more time, Lance, the clock is ticking, son." John tapped his Rolex. "Like I said last week, I ain't gonna wait patiently for that money to be returned to me. You're lucky you're still alive."

He spat food from between his teeth, then swept his hands around the garage. "And this here . . . your business—if that's what you wanna call it—if ya wanna see it still standin' an' not burned to the fuckin' ground, you'll get that money to me quick."

"John, please I—"

"No, Lance, we had a fuckin' deal, son."

John held out his hand as if ticking off a list, "I lent you the money you needed to get yourself out of the shit," he ticked off one of his stumpy nicotine-stained fingers, "and you repay me."

John ticked of his second finger, then raised it toward Lance, "if you can't keep your side of the deal, we all know where you'll end up, got it?"

"Yeah, yeah, chill out, John. I'll make a payment as soon as I can. Promise."

"You fuckin' better, or else."

Lance watched closely as John lit a cigarette. He spun around on his heels, then made his way to the entrance of the garage. Cars whooshed past the main road, during the early morning rush hour traffic. With his back turned to him, Lance kept an eye on John as he stood there. He kept one hand cocked inside his smart trouser suit pocket and the other, he raised slowly now and then as he smoked his cigarette.

"John, please, I really—"

"Shhh." John held up a hand and silenced him with his back still turned. "A deal's a deal, Lance." He looked over his shoulder. "I'm one of the most understanding loan sharks around London, you ask anyone. But I don't take too kindly to broken promises, fuck interest repayments."

He flicked his smoke on the pavement, turned to Lance and raised a hand to his ear. "The penalty for late payment is what, Lance?"

"Death."

Lance dropped his gaze to the ground and chewed on the inside of his lip. "I know John, like I said just give me—"

"Twenty-four hours Lance, you've been warned."

John flicked his wrist and glanced at the time. "Don't make me come back here cuz I don't wanna hear any of your bullshit excuses." He walked off towards his car.

Once he was out of sight, Lance let out a breath he didn't even realise he was holding. He shook his head, dropped the rag on the floor and headed over to his phone in his small back office. Hands shaking, he scrolled through his contracts, found who he was looking for, and then pressed call.

"Chelsea, it's me."

"Hi, Lance. What's up?"

"I need some money and quick."

"How much?"

"Hundred grand."

"A hundred grand! Lance, what the fuck have you got ya self into now? I ain't got that kinda—"

Lance moved the phone away from his ear and

paced his office. After a few rounds, he headed to the door and glanced outside.

No one was there, just the old clapped-out motor he was working on.

"Chelsea, don't lie," he said through gritted teeth into the phone.

"That old man left you everything. You've got access to that kind of money and ya know it."

"Let me think about it, okay?"

"What's there to think about Chelsea. We're together, we had a plan, I thought you'd help me out."

"What do you need it for?"

"I can't say right now, just do me this one favour will you?"

"I said I'd think about it, Lance, I need that money."

"Need it? Need it? Don't make me laugh, Chelsea, I need it in twenty-four hours."

"I'll think about it."

"Chelsea. Chelsea!"

The line disconnected. Lance dropped the phone on his messy desk, filled with paperwork and tools.

"Little bitch!"

. . .

Later that night, Lance turned on the gas fire burner on his grease-ridden stove, then rubbed his hands together over the heat to generate warmth. The unreliable heating system in the grubby one-bedroom flat he rented in a run-down area in Whitechapel, east London, hiccupped in the background.

His mind moved to John. "Twenty-four hours," he muttered, then turned to bang the central heating boiler on the wall, so it would click on.

Rolling his eyes, headed over to the table, and then picked up the past due bills he'd thrown down in a pile earlier. He rubbed his temples, but the stress continued to mount. With a deep sigh, he took a seat in front of the backlog of responsibilities he had abandoned months ago. As he did, out fell a newspaper clipping.

He snatched it up, narrowed his eyes, and then scanned over the headline.

"Millionaire found dead on the common."

He chuckled, straightened his face, then moulded it into a distorted, sinister smile.

Dropping the paper, he shifted through the unopened mail, all of which were red letters reminding him of the overdue payments on his business premises.

"Four months in debt, fuck! This can't be right."

He ran a hand over his stubbly chin, then fixed his eyes on the calendar on the wall.

"Has it really been that long?"

His phone buzzed with a text message.

John's name and a message floated across the top of his screen. He pulled up the text in full and read: Time's ticking, Lance. Twenty- four hours. Remember.

"Fuck you, John."

Closing the message, he scrolled back to Chelsea's name and pressed call. She answered on the first ring.

"What's up, Lance?"

"I need that money."

"You've not told me what for?"

"I just need it that's all. I'm behind on my mortgage payments, and I need a loan."

"A hundred grand worth of missed payments?" Chelsea laughed. "Do me a favour, Lance, I'm not that dumb—"

Lance gritted his teeth in frustration. "All right. Fine. Yes, I'm behind on my payments, but there's more to it. I took a loan from John Fuller to cover some other past debts I had, and now, I need to pay him back too."

"John Fuller, the local shark?"

"Yeah, you know him?"

"Who doesn't? You're in the shit if you can't pay him back. A few months ago, Pauly, you remember him, right? The bar owner from Bethnal Green, well, John strung him up by his balls from what I heard, all over late payments."

"You're not helping the situation, are you gonna give me the money? Yes or no?"

"Why didn't you use the money from John on your business debts?"

"I had to pay back an old score, one from a few years back I thought wouldn't catch up with me. There, now you know everything."

Lance got up from behind the table and headed over to the warmth of the gas burner. The heating system's full strength hadn't kicked in yet. London's weather had drastically changed over the last few days. One moment it felt like a mild autumn, the next, more like the harsh winter weather of January.

Lance lowered his voice, trying to keep himself composed. "Chelsea, listen, I thought we were a team?" Didn't we have a plan for that money together, once the old boy was gone?"

"Hmmm, yeah, that's the problem. I don't need a man who wants to live off my money."

Lance chuckled, and the sarcasm poured out of him. "Yeah, that's right. You prefer old millionaires about to kick the bucket, so you can scoop up all their cash, I forgot."

"Fuck you, Lance! I cared for Tony. You and his family can go to hell."

"Get a grip, woman. It was a joke. Where has your sense of humour gone? We both wanted the cash and him gone, remember. So really, you owe me."

"Owe you?" Lance heard the smirk in Chelsea's voice on the other end of the line.

"For what exactly? You didn't do shit. You were too scared to."

"Scared? I've been there, done that, and that's why I'm still in this shit hole of debt now. For not bumping off someone who I was paid to and taking the money. I don't want that life anymore," Lance yelled down the line.

"Whatever. Lance, bye."

"Chelsea, don't you dare put the—"

At the sound of the deadline, Lance threw his phone on the kitchen counter. He took a deep breath, licked his parched lips, and then racked his brain for his next move.

His gaze fell to the table holding his past due bills

and the newspaper cutting announcing Tony's death. Chelsea and his wife's pictures were beside an image of the dead millionaire. His eyes rested on Chelsea.

"You need teaching a lesson, girl. That money is as much mine as yours."

3

WHAT'S DONE IN THE DARK

Detective Dunne

Tuesday morning, Dunne and McDonald pulled up outside Chelsea Jackson's plush flat, overlooking London's River Thames.

"What do you think she pays for this?" Dunne brought the unmarked car to a slow crawl.

"More than she makes." McDonald glanced out the passenger side window.

The gated residential area, located a stone's throw from Vauxhall Bridge, was home to some of London's must sought after properties. Within walking distance from Victoria Station, yet it was close enough to commute into central London. But it was also within reaching distance of south

London's upmarket restaurants, bars, and cultural hot spots.

Dunne parked the car next to the curb, then did a quick visual sweep of the area.

McDonald, head bowed, double checked his notepad for details.

"Ready?" Dunne turned to McDonald.

"Yep. Number twenty-five, let's go." McDonald pocketed his notepad, then grabbed the car door handle.

Stepping out of the vehicle, Dunne rose to full height, working a cramp out of his calf, then stepped onto the pavement. He glanced at his watch. "It's ten thirty in the morning."

McDonald joined Dunne, and together, they headed over to the immaculate building.

"She might be at work." Dunne grabbed the handle of one of the glass double doors of the entrance and found it locked.

McDonald shrugged and pressed the intercom buzzer.

"Hello." A sleepy female voice answered.

"Miss Jackson, it's Detective McDonald. I'm here with Detective Dunne also."

"Huh, all right." A silent pause lingered, and then Chelsea yawned loudly into the intercom. "It's morning. How can I help you? detectives?"

We'd like to have a quick word with you, if that's okay?" McDonald leaned over the intercom box.

"Oh." Chelsea's voice jumped up an octave or two.

Dunne glanced at McDonald and whispered, "Well, that got her attention." The nervous tone of her voice replayed in his thoughts.

"Seems that way." McDonald nodded his head.

"W-what about?" Her voice cracked.

"If you could let us in, we won't keep you long," said McDonald in his most charming voice.

Buzzzzzzz.

At the sound of the doors unlocking, Dunne entered followed by McDonald.

Dunne glanced left then right. Nothing seemed out of place in the pristine entrance.

No doubt, the twenty-five flats were owned and rented by professionals, all with well-paid jobs. No urinated stairwells assaulted his nose. The corners remained rubbish free, and not a mark of graffiti lurked for the eyes to see.

"Come on." Dunne pushed through the entrance of the stairwell. "What was the number again?"

"Twenty-five." McDonald took the stairs two at a time.

Once on the floor, and in front of the door, McDonald rang the bell.

The door swung open, and a burst of lavender mixed with Jasmine, wafted from her flat.

"Morning." Chelsea, wrapped in a dressing gown with messy bedhead hair, leaned on the door frame.

"Morning, no work today?" Dunne ran his eyes over her, taking in her dishevelled appearance.

She looked like she had a late night. The dark circles under her eyes a tell-tale sign. Plus, her constant yawning. He glanced behind her into the flat, searching for any visitors she may have, but no one appeared to be there. There was no other lightening inside her home, and the curtains to the living area remained closed.

"No, it's my day off today."

A yawn escaped her lips, then she focused in closely on Dunne and his partner, as if taking in their suits and physique.

He and his partner were of similar height and build, but they had striking differences. Dunne's milk chocolate skin contrasted against his pale blue shirt, whereas McDonald's unusual mix of dark mahogany-coloured hair with icy blue eyes now seemed to hold her attention.

"Come in." She waved Dunne and his partner inside, then pointed behind her. "Go straight on into the living room."

Both Dunne and McDonald stepped over the

threshold, then made their way into the open plan living space.

Off to the left, Dunne visually took in an attached kitchen area—he cleared the room again visually, ruling out any additional occupants, then turned his attention to the living room.

Expensive, name brand leather sofas occupied the room.

A large television mounted on the wall was set to the ready position, and a perfect view of London filled the ceiling to floor windows.

Chelsea had gotten lucky when her late lover included her in his will, mused Dunne. He smoothed his beard and took in the sterile, almost picture-perfect book appearance of the area.

"Take a seat. I'll be with you in a minute."

Chelsea walked down a short hallway to what Dunne suspected was the bedroom.

McDonald took a seat, and Dunne joined him on the sofa.

Dunne leaned into his partner and whispered, "Wasn't this one of the properties he left her?"

"Yep. And from what I remember, it's just one of many."

"Damn, not bad," Dunne said under his breath, then took another look around. "Well, I can see why his family was so pissed she got everything."

"Exactly."

Dunne pondered the deceased millionaire's state of mind when he changed his will and cut his estranged wife and family out, leaving everything to a younger woman he had recently met.

"Two months he had a fling with her." McDonald checked his watch. "And she got everything?"

Chelsea appeared at the doorway dressed in a simple black dress. "So, what can I do for you gentlemen? Can I get you anything to drink?"

"No thanks," replied Dunne.

"Naw. I'm all good," said McDonald.

"We have a few questions for you." Dunne decided to just dive in since he didn't have all day.

4

DE JA VU

Chelsea

Chelsea lowered herself onto the sofa opposite Dunne and McDonald, then covered her face with her hands.

"Not this again. I thought we were done. I've not done anything. I have no idea—"

"Look, Chelsea, we understand that," replied Dunne. "His murder was closed and left as a cold case. But we have a few more questions for you. Something else has come to light."

Chelsea's gaze flashed back to meet Dunne's dark brown eyes in an instant.

What? She gripped the hem of her skirt, then smoothed the fabric over her thighs.

Dunne's words caused her pulse to race for a second, but she recovered and focused on getting her body language in check. She remained cautious, not wanting to appear on edge by the unexpected news.

Chelsea remembered all too well how observant Dunne and his little side kick were, especially during the last investigation into Tony's murder. The last thing she needed was to be in the spotlight, again.

She didn't relish being under the thumbs of the detectives or for Tony's family to examine her life under a microscope.

Her mind briefly moved to Manisha—Tony's estranged but very legal wife.

This can't be happening! I bet she's behind all this, she thought.

She tossed the situation around in her mind as if to try and place exactly what could have come to light that would send Dunne back to her doorstep. Her fear turned to rage.

A steady heat pooled in her stomach and made its way through her body, invoking her anger. The mere thought of Tony's family, or anyone else for that matter, messing up her plans again didn't settle well.

Chelsea took a deep breath, smoothed over her

hair, then fixed the most innocent face for Dunne and McDonald she could muster.

She placed a hand over her heart and got into character as if to resume her delegated role to remain off Dunne's radar.

"What do you mean something else has come to light?" She widened her eyes and glanced from Dunne to McDonald. "Do we have more information on who killed Tony?"

Her hand fell to her cheek, then she strained out a few tears. "I still can't believe it. Who would have done such a thing?" Her words slipped past her lips through false sobs and tears. "He had no enemies as far as I knew."

"We need to talk to you at the station." McDonald scooted to the edge of the sofa, his knees pressing against the coffee table.

"Wait." Chelsea shifted her wide-eyed gaze back to him. "Are you arresting me again?"

She wiped at her eyes with the back of her hand, playing the hurt, vulnerable lover, yet, inside, she seethed. The heat of anger threatened to explode and mess up the hard work she had done throughout the last investigation to claim her innocence.

Dunne's stare roamed over her as if he were studying her carefully.

Chelsea ignored him, sniffled, dabbed at her tears, and then met McDonald's ice blue eyes.

"More like an interview—under caution." McDonald held her gaze.

"But I've not—"

"Just come with us to the station, Chelsea, then you're free to enjoy the rest of your day." McDonald moved a decretive pillow, setting it at the end of the couch.

Chelsea rose and looked around her home. She took in the luxury surrounding her and kicked herself for not booking a one way ticketed to Australia sooner. Big plans were in the work that required the money sitting in her account. And they didn't involve Lance, these detectives, or any of Tony's surviving family members.

Holding back a smile, she felt it bubble within her. The thought of the vision board she had made and displayed in her bedroom kept her focused on the task at hand. Her goal was to set herself up with a nice little place near the beach somewhere in Australia, forget about working, and do something she enjoyed with her life. Like painting, it was her one true talent other than number crunching as an accountant. Numbers paid well, but not well enough for the life she wanted. Plus, London's weather was nothing exciting. She figured she could more than afford to take some time out, work on her tan, and find herself a nice Australian hunk to pass the time.

She glared at McDonald and tried to steady her breathing. "This isn't fair. We went through all this before I—"

"Let's go." McDonald rose to his feet, followed by Dunne.

Both men stood towering over her.

Peeking from under her lashes, she looked at them. They didn't scare her. She only hoped her innocent act would wash with one or both of them. Sure, she had a motive for Tony's death, but so did his wife—she reminded herself of this.

Focus on the here and now, she thought.

The heavy gaze of Dunne and McDonald thickened the air.

"Why can't you ask me whatever you want here?"

"Interviews under caution need to be recorded—you know this," Dunne said.

Chelsea sized him up, moving her eyes over his lean frame. Dunne seemed impatient to her, she sensed it. And if she wasn't mistaken, he wanted to hurry up the process.

Only one issue made her skin crawl. At the station, the detectives could cross examine her, then playback her responses, searching for holes. She was well aware of this, and that made her nervous. The thought of her personal life put on display again, brought a sense of dread to rest heavy on her chest. But she didn't want them to know how she felt or that she was trying to stay one step ahead. She must remain careful with all that she said and did, including her mannerisms and facial expressions.

"Recorded, yeah." Chelsea threw her head back and laughed. "How can I forget. Give me a second, I'll grab a jacket."

Chelsea knew then that her hunch was right. He did want to speed up the process.

"Make it quick." Dunne let out an impatient breath and shot a side-glance at his partner.

She turned to leave the room, contemplating what to wear—a coat, cloak, or wool wrap.

Footsteps tapped against the wooden floor behind her. Chelsea glanced over a shoulder just in time to catch sight of McDonald peeking into her kitchen.

Pausing for a moment at her bedroom door, she listened to the men's conversation. Their voices remained low, floating out of the main living area.

"This is gonna be a headache, I can tell," whispered McDonald.

"Yeah, but if we don't at least follow up on the evidence, who knows what we'll miss." Dunne stepped into view. "Or what we've already missed."

She crept forward, slightly, then watched Dunne, who now stood in front of the circular mirror, smoothing his tie.

Evidence? She covered her mouth to stem the gasp that almost escaped. What evidence? Her mind raced back and forth over the last investigation. There was no evidence, well not enough, anyway. Otherwise, they never would have closed the case, marking it unsolved.

She mused further over the information flowing through her thoughts, then backed into her room, gently closing the door. Back against the frame, she wrapped her arms around herself. A frown of frustration hit her lips.

She sighed deeply, chewing on the skin around her thumb nail.

Chelsea headed over to her dresser, grabbed her phone, then checked for messages—there were none.

On autopilot she pulled up Lance's name and typed out a message. She thought twice about it, and then deleted the message.

Slowly, she turned around from her dresser and pondered her next move.

"Chelsea," Dunne's voice called out.

She jumped to attention. "Just give me a second, I'm coming."

Tension tightened the muscles in her neck and

back. She made her way over to the large wardrobe stuffed with designer clothes and shoes and freed a black jacket from a hanger. Quickly, she slid it over her frame and closed the door.

In the mirror on the back of the wardrobe's doorframe, she looked herself in the eye. "You've got this!"

Pep talk over, she grabbed her handbag from beside the bed, shoved her phone inside a corner pocket of the bag, then made her to the door.

She placed a hand on the knob, then paused a moment. Her shoulders sagged, rolling forward. A grieving expression masked her face, and she let out a calming breath, preparing for her role. Once in character, she made her way out to Detective Dunne and McDonald.

5

ONE STEP AHEAD

Detective Dunne

One hour later, back at the police station, Dunne and McDonald sat opposite of Chelsea in the interview room.

Dunne pressed record on the audio device and double checked the cameras were rolling.

"This is Detective Dunne, present with me is Detective McDonald. This interview is being carried out in Interview Room One." He paused a moment. "For the purpose of this recording, please confirm your name."

"Chelsea Jackson."

"Date of birth, Miss Jackson." Dunne glanced at her.

"Twentieth of March 1983."

"Chelsea, as mentioned, this interview is part of an enquiry into the death of your late boyfriend, Mr. Patel—"

"I understand. Can we just get this over with? I've got nothing to hide. I've always wanted to find his murderer."

"Fair enough." Dunne reached for the remote control on the table. "Take a look at this." He pressed play and watched Chelsea's reaction closely.

A red blush rose up her neck and touched her cheeks. Her eyes moved over the screen, then she sucked in a gasp as if in shock. For a second, a deep frown covered her lips and a perfectly arched brow cocked toward the screen. The vulnerable, innocent girl look she wore vanished, replaced by a poker face. Her chest rose and fell deeply, she narrowed her eyes and stared off into space, averting her eyes from the screen.

Dunne loved this part, when a suspect realised he was one step ahead of them. He took full advantage and tried to break her down further.

"Chelsea, you okay?" He asked.

Sarcasm dripped from his response, "looks like a pretty intimate moment you were having there, but that's not Tony is it?"

Dunne noticed her energy shift from the grief-stricken girlfriend to pissed off—it was tangible. He focused in on Chelsea for a moment as she stared off into space and avoided his eye contact. Visibly he noticed her try to control her breathing. He watched the muscles of her jaws twitch, then she grinded her teeth together.

Images of her and an unknown man in a car moved over the screen. In the visual scene, Chelsea's head dipped low into the man's lap. He moved his focus from the video back to her, Chelsea rolled her eyes and exhaled a long sigh.

Dunne adjusted his chair to lean back. There was no mistake over what was taking place in the recording. The camera became unsteady as it zoomed in slightly, and the man in the car grabbed a handful of Chelsea's hair, pulling her head up from his lap, then kissed her. Once the kiss ended, Chelsea straddled the man's lap. Dunne shifted his eyes from the scene back to Chelsea.

She let out yet another frustrated breath, then drummed the already worn wooden table with her manicured fingernails.

"Switch it off," she said, "I've seen enough."

Dunne let the video play on for a moment longer and observed her while she fidgeted in her chair, she stopped drumming her nails on the table. Instead, she chewed the skin around her nails. A habit he thought was disgusting but recognised as a tell-tale sign she was about to break. He wrinkled his nose, then moved his gaze over her further, and noticed her right leg bounced up and down, he felt the vibration against the table.

"I said, switch it off!" Chelsea's voice bellowed around the small interview room,

"where the hell did you get that?"

Dunne ignored her question. He flipped open his notepad to check his notes. McDonald paused the tape and took over the interview.

"Chelsea, for the purpose of the tape recording," McDonald pointed to the screen, "can you confirm who that is in the video footage?"

Dunne watched her closely he noted that, Chelsea shifted her pinched-up expression from the screen, over to face him. She sat upright, chewed the inside of her lip, then moved her gaze back and forth between him and McDonald, as if she tried to read them. Dunne remained emotionless on purpose. His poker face gave nothing away.

To Dunne as he took a back seat and let his partner call the shots, it appeared that her brain was ticking. She straightened her back, opened her mouth as if to talk then closed it.

"Well, let me explain," she started, "that was me. And . . . he, uhm . . . that's a f-friend of mine."

"A friend?"

McDonald questioned as he rose an eyebrow in her direction. "Chelsea, according to the date of this recording you were in a relationship with Tony Patel. He turned up dead three days later."

Dunne bit his lip in anticipation of her excuses as he noticed Chelsea fiddle with the hem on the sleeve of her jacket across the table. She twisted the material tightly around her fingers.

"Yes, we were together."

She responded as she blushed then looked away from McDonald's intense gaze.

"Chelsea, in your own words what took place in that car between you and this man?" McDonald continued.

"We had sex, okay. Yes! We had sex."

"So, who is he?"

"A friend."

"Name?"

"Why what does this have to do with anything? You need to focus on finding Tony's murderer not who I had a two second fling with!"

Dunne glanced at his partner, McDonald's ice blue eyes were trained on Chelsea, "name, please Chelsea." He pushed on and ignored her comments.

"Lance Duncan, he owns a garage near my office. One day my car broke down and we got talking."

Dunne noted down the name and returned his glance to Chelsea. "You mean you were more than friends, by the looks of it?" Dunne nodded in the direction of the frozen video clip on the screen showing Chelsea straddling the man. Chelsea shifted in her chair nervously, every move she made Dunne scrutinised.

"Yes. You could say so."

"How long were you seeing Lance?" Dunne asked.

She glanced back at the screen.

He noticed the hesitation in her response and waited.

The corner of her mouth twisted to one side. She looked at her lap, glanced from him to McDonald, then lowered her lashes, again.

Dunne took a deep breath to keep his patience in check. "Chelsea, can you answer the question please?"

"Chelsea, if you could please answer the question." He pushed her again.

"About a month or so."

"Why the affair? You assured us before you were both happy." McDonald questioned.

"Yes, we were happy, I did love him, I still do. It just happened one of those things. Lance knew about Tony's cancer and wanted us to be together once he passed away."

"So, what are you saying? You had free will, you didn't have to continue the affair."

"I know. It just happened."

"Have you seen him since?"

Chelsea paused, bit the inside of her lip, then shifted her eyes from McDonald to the table.

"Well, no. I mean yes, but not like that."

"When did you last see him?"

"I can't remember."

"Chelsea, think back." Dunne sighed impatiently.

Chelsea glanced at the ceiling, and after a beat, she met Dunne's gaze. "A few weeks back, I've not seen him since."

"All right, for now we have no more questions." McDonald glanced over at Dunne, who nodded in agreement.

"For now?" Chelsea's eyes widened. "You mean you don't believe me? It was just a fling that got out of hand."

McDonald reached over and switched off the audio recording. "For now, you're free to go," he told her.

Chelsea stared blankly at the screen with the video paused, then rose to her feet.

"I didn't do it. What they all think I did. I would never, I loved Tony."

Chelsea broke down in tears. "He was still legally married, but we fell in love." She sobbed. "His wife and family hate me, but I didn't force him to change his will in my favour when I learned about his cancer."

Dunne eyed Chelsea closely, then pulled out a box of tissues from the desk drawer.

"Here, wipe your eyes. Just stay calm and head home." He handed her a Kleenex. "We'll be in contact if anything further comes up."

"Okay." Chelsea sniffed, then blew her nose. "Thank you, Detective."

6

I SPY

Chelsea

Chelsea approached the reception desk of the police station to collect her things.

"Sign here," said the female officer on duty.

She wrote her name, signed, then picked up the clear plastic bag containing her belongings.

In a huff, she placed one hand on the door handle, exited the police station, and stepped out onto the pavement. She glanced around, not sure what she expected to find.

Swiftly, she walked to her car and got inside. Once seated, she blew out a frustrated breath, then massaged her temples.

"Think, think." She examined the damage around

her thumbnail from chewing around the edges under Dunne's hawk like gaze.

She pulled out her phone, then scrolled through her contacts.

Lance's name in bold text stood out on the screen. A sense of paranoia came over her. It was almost as if his name itself mocked her for the situation she had found herself in for the second time.

Chelsea moved her thumb over his name on the screen.

Three months ago, when Tony's body had turned up on the common in the local park, it had been a surprise to her, yes. But she'd be lying if she said she wasn't happy.

"You were good to me, Tony. But you weren't Mr. Right—just the Mr. Right for now."

She laughed out loud, then muted herself with a serious expression.

Scrolling past Lance's name, she landed on Manisha Patel's contact details—his legal wife's name.

A twisted smile and a small chuckle escaped her lips. She threw her phone in her bag, started the car's engine, and then took off towards her home.

Thirty minutes later, Chelsea shut off the engine on the quiet road and glanced at her watch. It was only mid-day.

She sat a few houses down from where Manisha's car was parked, outside what was once the marital home of Manisha and Tony.

What am I even doing here, again? Every now and then, she had driven past the property to keep tabs on what Manisha was up to, especially during the battle over Tony's Last Will in Testament.

Nothing ever looked out of place, and to her surprise, she hadn't put the house up for sale to try to claw back some of the money—according to Manisha—the woman felt she had been robbed of.

A figure made its way out of the gate of the house. It was Manisha.

Chelsea ducked down slightly, keeping her whereabouts a secret.

Manisha got into a car and took off in the opposite direction.

"That was close."

Chelsea chuckled, half-startled and half-intrigued by where Manisha could be on her way to. Curiosity got the better her. So, she started the engine and pulled out of the parking space.

"Nah." She decided against that course of action. "I'll check on you some other time, Manisha."

Chelsea did a three-point turn on the quiet road and headed back the way she came, away from Manisha's home.

SNEAK PEEK OF SACRIFICES

Sacrifices is a riveting romantic story with historical and suspenseful elements set in the 1960s jazz scene and the present day.

Jane O'Sullivan, a sultry twenty-seven-year-old singer, starts a torrid, forbidden affair during the 1960s jazz scene in London. Working hard, she makes a name for herself. She's a woman with dreams, hopes, and a burning desire to leave Europe behind and travel to New Orleans with her lover, Louis.

Louis Simpson, a charming twenty-nine-year-old musician from Jackson, Mississippi, is on tour with his band in London. Back home, the height of the civil rights movement plays out in the USA. Driven by ambition, a forbidden love, and a desire to turn his life around, he pushes forward, living his dream.

Once their paths cross, a twist of fate crushes Jane's world, forcing her to make a life-changing decision that impacts both her and Louis. This historical love story spans across the Atlantic and roams through Europe with love, loss, and broken promises.

Twenty-five years later, when Jane and Louis' paths cross on a Greek Island, will the helping hand of fate bring them together, or rip them apart, once more?

1

MEMORIES

Summer, 2019, Atlanta, USA

Damn . . . 1960. It seems like just yesterday. Amazing, how one picture holds so many other memories attached to it.

"Nanna." From behind the bedroom door, Javan's husky voice floats through the air. "Are you there?"

Running the side of her hand along the middle of the half-slip, she creates a crease. She folds the garment into a four-inch square, then tucks it into the corner of the dresser.

"I know you're there."

A single tear rolls down Jane's cheek. Using her hip, she closes the drawer.

The bedroom door creaks open. "I'm coming in, okay?"

She rolls her eyes, then sighs. Rubbing her temples, she brushes away tears with the back of a hand, then reaches for a tissue.

Javan enters the room, closing the door behind him.

Ignoring him, she moves to the window, overlooking the large pool in the back courtyard.

The gardeners tend to his beloved flower beds, just like they have done since the 80s. The employees often change, but the routine never does. He had insisted the area remained a picture of beauty. It made him feel like he was home, rather than holed up in a Las Vegas hotel.

"Please, tell me what's on your mind, Nanna?"

Jane glances at him with uncertainty but says nothing.

"What's up?" Javan peers out the window, then turns his full attention to her. "You look like you've seen a ghost."

"Nothing, it's"—she rolls the tissue between her fingers—"well, not really. You just look like him. You've got his long lashes, hair, his brown eyes, his mocha skin. Everything about you reminds me of him."

"So, tell me about him."

With a huff, and under Javan's intense gaze, Jane gives in.

"I miss him." She pats his arm. "Nothing can be done about it though."

"I know, come here." Pulling Jane into his arms, he cradles her. "It's okay."

Resting her head on his chest, eyes closed, she inhales traces of his fresh aftershave—a gift she had given him a few weeks ago for his birthday.

"Nanna, you never told me how you two met. I know you guys had a lot of history, but, well, if I'm about to take over, I need to understand him. I want to do this right."

"No honey, not today." Pushing him away, Jane wriggles from his embrace. "I don't want to go that far back."

"I know it's hard. It's only been six months since he died. We'll get through it together. Please tell me about him."

"It's painful." Jane caresses the picture, then sniffles. "He was here one moment laughing and joking, then the next, he was fighting for his life. The doctor said his liver disease was under control, I just don't—"

A soft sob escapes her lips, and she shudders.

"Shh, it's okay, c'mon. Let me take the photo for

you." He places it on the edge of the dresser scarf, propping it up against a perfume bottle.

Wrapping an arm around her shoulders, he guides her to the bed.

"Here we go. Take a seat. Tell me all about him." Raising an eyebrow at her, it's as if Javan tries to encourage her to open up. "The actual story Nanna, not the fairy-tale. Tell me what I'm getting myself in to. You know, filling his shoes and all?"

Laughing, Jane squeezes his hand. "You'll do just fine, like I said, it was so long ago that we met. Things were complicated back then."

"Fine, tell me the history of Rhythm Records then. What do I need to know? What about the music? That's always been your passion and his."

Leaning her head to one side in deep thought at the mention of her all-time love, Jane picks up her reading glasses from the nightstand.

"We're going to go back to a time, way back. To a time, you weren't even thought of yet. A time I never even thought I'd be a grandmother." Jane gazes at him in a dreamy haze. "Go get the photo album on the top shelf." She points in the general direction. "And prepare yourself because this isn't a tale for the squeamish at heart."

2

FAREWELL

London, 1985

Jane heads toward Westminster Bridge. Her fit pump walking shoes tap against the sidewalk.

It's a busy Monday morning in central London. People walk the streets with a brisk stride on their way to work or to shop. Energetic joggers dodge cars and cyclists at traffic lights and corners.

Bright sunshine lights the day, and a cool breeze caresses her face. She swings an arm back and forth, and with the other, she holds a disposable drink tray with two steamy, hot cups of cappuccino. A fresh aroma tickles her nose.

Approaching the foot of the bridge, she stops at

the pedestrian crossing, then gazes across the view of the capital.

"Nothing like London's rush hour," she mumbles under her breath.

Black taxis speed past. Red double-decker buses, full of city workers commuting to office buildings, move down the bus lane.

The traffic light turns green, and commuters move about with their day.

A gust scatters fluffy clouds across a blue sky. The sun peeks out, kissing her cheeks with warm rays.

Mindful of a cyclist rounding the corner on his bike at full speed, she waits, then crosses the street. Once safely across, her pace increases to a full-speed power walk along the bridge.

A new spring in her step got her out of bed earlier than usual this morning.

Finally, her time has come. Four weeks' ago, Jane had handed in her application, requesting an early retirement. Now in her fifties, and with careful saving and financial planning, she has decided it is time for her to wind down and enjoy life.

Working for London's Royal Mail postal service started out as a part-time job. Something to put food on the table and a roof over her head. Back then, it gave her ample time to focus on her dream to make it big as a jazz singer, in the late 50s. She had made plans, and she was going places. But that was a long time ago.

Life changes, the thought comes to mind, *and before you know it, dreams fade into the backdrop of work.*

The red and white Royal Mail logo comes into view. Stopping dead in her tracks, and eyeing the building, Jane takes in the minor details overlooked.

Her gaze roams over the brickwork and small windows, tinted with dirt from London's polluted air. The deep cut architectural lines brimming each story of the structure catch her eye.

Hmm. Have they always been there?

She bites her lip, then narrows her eyes.

Twenty-odd years gone by in a blink. I'll miss this place. At last, I can rediscover what I love in life.

Sipping the last of her coffee, she turns her back on the building. Her vision rests on Trafalgar Square's pavement outside the office. With five minutes to spare, she walks over to the low brick wall, then takes a seat.

What will my new routine be like after retirement? A nervous energy makes her fidget. *No, you can do this, pull yourself together.*

Taking a deep breath, she gathers herself together and puts her best foot forward.

Entering the office, Jane flashes her ID badge.

"Top of the morning, Jane." The security officer, John, nods with a smile, and takes the offered cup of coffee.

"Morning." Once he scans her in, she heads toward the lift.

At her desk, she settles down, then shuffles through her diary planner and paperwork, preparing for the day.

"Good morning." Rita, her co-worker and one of her closest girlfriends, approaches with two cups of tea.

"One of those better be for me?"

"You know it is." Placing the cups on Jane's desk, Rita sits on a chair next to her. "How are you this morning? Last day."

"Umm, I can hardly believe it myself."

"How are you feeling?"

Jane lets out a breath, and studies her friend's face, admiring her long, black hair pulled into a single braid low at her nape. Her Asian-Indian genes keep her looking young and wrinkle free.

"Part of me feels good"—Jane pauses in thought—"the other half remains paralysed with fear." She runs a hand through her blonde, bobbed hair.

"Fear?" Rita raises her arms overhead. "Of what?" The gold bangles jingle on her wrists, reminding her of tambourines. "You have a whole new life to live. Well, now that you're not stuck to the shackles of this place."

Jane takes in the drab looking office. "Hmm, I guess so. It's been so many years."

"It has been. But it's your time now." Rita gives her arm a quick squeeze. "I'm so jealous. I have another two years to wait until I can apply for an early retirement."

Chuckling at the small talk, Jane nods to co-workers making their way into the office.

Her department has become overrun with younger, career-driven women.

"Psst." Rita nudges Jane with an elbow to the ribs, then nods toward Sandra or 'Sandy' as she likes to be called—the new office supervisor standing by the photocopier.

Sandy's business dress shows just the right amount of feminine sexiness. High-heels, bare legs, a fitted skirt and suit jacket with extra thick shoulder pads. The ensemble screams, 'I'm going somewhere, so get out of my way.'

Jane draws in a deep breath. "Hmm." She turns to Rita as if reading her friend's mind. "I remember those days."

"Me, too. Boy, do I miss them. But we've still got it. They say fifty is the new forty, right?"

"Ha. She's barely in her thirties. But you're right, we still got it."

Giggling, Rita turns back in Sandy's direction and an awkward silence falls between them.

"Anyway"—Jane breaks the speechless contemplation—"I better get going. I'm on the service desk this morning. I'll catch up with you at lunchtime."

"Sure, I'll see you then."

Downstairs, seat adjusted at the counter, Jane greets the day, ready for the morning rush of customers. Her line snakes well beyond the usual pathway.

Wow, a queue already. It's going to be a busy day.

Over twenty years behind the counter, she can do the job with her eyes closed, and with one hand tied behind her back.

A tall, handsome man—young enough to be her son—confidently makes his way toward her from the other side of the counter.

Oh, my, that suit. Back in the day, she recalls a few memories that flash before her eyes. *Men used to dress sharp—care about their appearance.*

He drops a package on the counter.

"Mornin', ma'am. This is going first class to Canada." Tilting his head to one side, he narrows his eyes at Jane. "Are you okay? You look faint."

"Oh, I'm sorry. I was in my own little world.

What is it you wanted, love? Postage to the United States of America, did you say?"

"No, Canada." The young man smiles at Jane as if to humour her tardiness. "Close enough though."

"Yes. Straight away." Jane organises his package. Her mind drifts to a place she hadn't allowed herself to go for a while . . . *Maurice's Place, Oxford Street, Central London, 1960.*

A spotlight warms the stage. Curtains, attached to the rafters, cascade to the hardwood floor. The roar of applause filters to her ears.

"Thank you, ladies an' gentlemen." Jane's broad east London accent rings out across the room. "That's very kind of you."

Wow, she thinks, what a night. A dream come true.

Her eyes flash to the left of the stage.

Two women deep in conversation over her performance catch her attention. They look up at her.

One leans into the other and says behind a hand, "That voice of hers, it's amazing."

"Hmm, and the dress"—the taller of the two chimes in —"I love the Ivory colour."

"Yeah. I bet it's expensive." The woman of shorter stature wiggles her fingers. "Love the red nails too, complements her lipstick, don't you think?"

Focus Jane, focus, the self-talk rattles in her brain.

Jane moves her attention away from the gossiping ladies and beams a wide smile at the crowd.

The competition for work is fierce these days, especially with the influx of talent from overseas to the United Kingdom (UK). Powerful voices from every corner of the world make their way into the few jazz houses London has. Mainly newcomers from the Caribbean, snap up the invitation to the UK, with the promise of a British passport and citizenship, to help with the skills' shortage employers face, post-war.

Many of the immigrants must work mundane day jobs to make a living but performing on stage and jazz in general are their genuine passions and reasons for relocating overseas.

A saxophone rhythm kicks in, crooning a soothing beat.

Jane takes a deep breath. She lets out the first line of her next song in a deep, sultry voice into the microphone. Her voice travels around the room.

The crowd moves their attention to centre stage, where she stands under a spotlight.

This is where I belong, she thinks to herself, soaking up the attention from the crowd, right here on stage.

Her blonde hair and blue eyes deceive many, a fact she has known almost all her life. Spectators never expect to hear a husky, soulful voice when she opens her mouth.

The 'Blue-Eyed Lady of Jazz' had become her new pet

name around London's jazz scene. Well, once she had proved her ability to sing all the famous hits with heart and do them justice.

"Miss," a distant voice carries Jane out of her daydream. "Ma'am, are you sure you're all right?"

Jane focuses her attention to the present, and the customer at her counter.

"Oh, I'm so sorry." She places an extra strip of tape down the middle of the package. "I don't know what has come over me this morning."

"It's okay. So, how much is it to get this off to Canada?"

"That'll be ten pounds. Ten-twenty, please, love."

The young man pulls out a wallet, then hands her a £20.00 note.

"Out of £20"—on autopilot once again, she hands him change—"here you go."

"You have a good day now."

"Thanks, you too." A smile dances across her lips. "By the way, you look great in your suit. Knock em' dead."

"I'll do that." The man laughs, waves goodbye, then turns to leave the counter.

Jane's eyes follow him out the door.

If only you knew what a suit like that meant to me years ago, she thinks to herself.

It feels like minutes, rather than hours, since Jane

first sat behind the customer service desk. She glances at the enormous clock over the entrance of the post office's door.

Uh-oh, where's the time gone this morning, the words echo in her mind. *Lunch time already?*

Rising, she leaves her perch behind the counter, makes her way to the stairs, then takes the lift to the sixth floor.

In the hallway, voices drift her way. She rounds the corner, then enters the open floor plan office. Her gaze zooms in on her desk in the centre of the room.

Flowers, cards, and various chocolates garnish her desk.

Wow, so sweet of them.

Heading farther into the room, she wipes her eyes.

Party poppers go off behind her, making her jump.

Rita, Paul, Sandy, and a few other co-workers she knows by face, rather than name, call out 'Surprise, Jane' in unison.

"Oh, my. You gave me a fright." Hand to her chest, the flutter of her heart beats like 16th notes on a musical score. "Have you got any idea how fragile my heart is? You nearly gave me a heart attack."

"Nonsense." A smile blooms from ear to ear on

Sandy's face. "There's life in you yet. So, don't talk such rubbish. Come 'er and give us a hug." Sandy embraces Jane in a tight bear hug, not giving her time to object.

"Thank you, dear."

"You're welcome. Are you ready to head out for lunch? We've reserved half the restaurant down at Mr. Liu's Chinese, especially for you." She winks, then slips the strap of her purse over a shoulder. "Grab 'ya jacket, let's go."

Jane looks at Sandy with teary eyes. *Maybe I had her wrong, after all?*

3

IT'S A NEW DAWN, A NEW DAY

THE SECOND HAND of the clock ticks to 5:30 p.m., and a buzzer sounds the end of the workday.

After the emotional final farewell luncheon with her co-workers, which took up most of her afternoon, Jane tidies her desk and pulls on her fit pumps.

Well, this is it, my last commute home.

The image of the young man she served this morning has stayed with her all day, pulling her back to her youth and the time she had spent on stage.

What a lovely young man, she thinks to herself. *I wonder where he works. And that suit, my, my, my.*

Powering down her computer for the last time, brings about a bit of nostalgia. She takes in the room once more, memorising it in great detail, then gathers the flowers and gifts she had received earlier.

The voices and comments of her co-workers run through her mind: life has just started. There is plenty to see and do. You're not over the hill, Jane. Enjoy your time, it's yours now.

Her eyes well with tears, then she breaks down into an uncontrollable sob. A quick glance around the office confirms she remains alone.

Arms full of trinkets and gifts, she heads toward the lift.

On the ground floor, she ambles to the security desk with her badge. She looks down at the picture taken years ago.

Retired, that's my title now.

"Here you go." Handing in her ID badge at the security desk, she forces a smile across her face. "Bye, John, take care, love." She chokes back a sob. "It was lovely working with you."

John glances over his screen at her from his desk. "Jane, I'll miss you." A wide smile breaks out across his normally serious face. "Who's gonna bring my morning coffee now?"

She giggles softly, burning to memory the smile on his face and the kindness in his eyes.

"No, seriously, you'll be missed. It's been great getting to know you over the years."

"You too. Now, come here"—she extends her arms, inviting him to a hug—"in all these years, I've never seen you come out from behind that desk."

John blushes but walks into Jane's waiting arms. She squeezes his large six-foot-three frame.

"Have fun." He leans into her embrace. "In a way, I envy you."

"Why is that?"

"I've got at least another thirty years until my time."

Jane looks at the youthful man young enough to be her son, then smiles.

"That's what everyone keeps saying. I'll try my best." She hugs him one last time. "All the best, love."

John releases Jane and leans over his desk to open the security gates for her.

"Take care." With a final wave, she sets off and leaves Royal Mail Post Office for the last time.

Outside, the early evening air is a few degrees cooler than it was during the day. Commuters crowd the streets and sidewalks, brushing past her in a rush.

All these people, it's so busy.

Turning off Trafalgar Square, she walks along Pall Mall toward Westminster Bridge.

Next to the mall, a familiar sound meets her ears, and she slows her pace.

A saxophone? My gosh, she thinks to herself, *I've not heard a live player in years.*

Her feet pull her toward the crowd outside the pub.

In the corner, a tall, tattily dressed black man with dark glasses plays a serious jazz tune.

The crowd cheers and drops small change into the hat in front of him.

In the background, she eases a comfortable distance from the people gathered around, and enjoys the scene unfolding.

Lost in the melody, the musician seems to become one with the music. His foot taps along with the steady cadence, and his frame sways to the beat of the piece.

The rifts of the talented player hypnotise Jane. A small bench close to the crowd catches her eye. She settles herself on the smooth surface and listens.

A long sigh escapes her lips.

Retired. Free to do what I want. No real responsibilities. No routine. No work. No one special.

Reflecting on the reality of her impending new normal, she chews the side of her lip. The excitement she had felt handing in her badge for the last time fights for her attention.

Twenty-five years ago, she would have never

imagined she would spend her life in London, behind a Royal Mail's counter.

I had ambition, dreams, the words haunt her. *I was born to be a star.* She sighs once more. *But it all ended when I met him.*

4

MAURICE'S PLACE

Oxford Street, Central London, 1960

Lifting the hem of her elegant black dress, Jane steps down from the stage.

The crowd cheer, clap, and beg for more sultry tunes.

Wow. I need a break, she muses to herself. *My voice won't last the week at this rate.*

She just gave them all she had, singing a heartfelt version of Smokey Robinson's *Who's Loving You?*

Moving confidently through the crowd, heads turn in her direction, and smiles come her way. Through the smoke-filled room she heads to the bar, then takes a seat.

"You did great up there, Jane." Jenelle pats the seat next to her. "You sounded amazin'."

"Thanks, that means so much coming from you."

Jenelle playfully laughs, then places an arm around Jane's shoulders. "I mean it, don't sell ya'self short. You should seriously think 'bout comin' back with us to New Orleans. We could do with a blue-eyed, soulful sister on board."

A bartender slides a dry martini between Jane and Jenelle.

Wow, this treatment, she chuckles to herself. *I could get used to it.*

Jane takes a sip from the glass. Pondering Jenelle's proposal, she extracts a thin smoke, then places it in the holder.

Jenelle fires a match. "Need a light?"

"Thanks." Drawing the smoke deep into her lungs, Jane leans back, then looks around.

The jazz room is dimly lit with soft lighting. Dark oak tables, with red fabric-lined chairs and sofas face the stage, and a combination of chairs, stools, and benches line the walls around the room.

Whisky and cigars fill the air.

The bar Jane is sitting at, has a high, glossy polish, thanks to Jenelle's watchful eye. She wipes every drip of liquor and flick of ash customers drop.

On the stage, a black piano, a microphone stand, and a set of drums rest, ready for each act.

Maurice's Place feels like home now, after seven years.

At sixteen, she had left school with good qualifications, then bummed around for four years between Dublin, Ireland, and London deciding what to do with her life.

At twenty, she scored her first on-stage role at Maurice's Place, working behind the bar three nights a week and singing the other two. Now twenty-seven years old, the atmosphere of Maurice's Place, and the variety of customers have kept her here. The chilled out, low-key bar attracts the clientele she enjoys performing for.

Jane inhales her smoke, then glances around. The jazz scene in London is picking up, but New Orleans would be like a dream come true.

The lights in the room lower, and the spotlight moves to the stage, hushing the crowd. Men and women relax in the comfy sofas and chairs around the tables. All eyes move to the centre of the room.

Three men set themselves on the stage: a lead singer, a saxophone player, and a piano player. The smooth vocals of the male lead, floats through the air.

Wow. Who is that?

She studies the saxophone player. His skilful fingers move over his instrument.

"So, what do-ya say Jane?"

The corner of Jenelle's lips turn up slowly at Jane, who remains under the spell of the musicians on stage.

Jane's eyes stay trained on the saxophone player. Her smoke has long reached the end, yet it is poised between her fingers.

Laughing to herself, Jenelle waves a hand in front of Jane, as if to snap her out of a daze.

"Earth to Jane. Earth to Jane. Anyone home?"

"Gosh, I'm sorry. I didn't catch what you said?"

"Look at you. All caught up in the music, or is it Mr. Sax player?"

Jane moves her gaze away from the stage and joins in the girly laughter with her friend.

Dropping her burned out smoke in the ashtray, she reaches for another one, then turns to Jenelle "Wow, he is handsome, don't you think?"

"More than handsome. He sure can play, too."

"Hmm, I've never seen this band before, have you?"

"Not here, no. But they've played over at Ronnie's a few times. I was over there just last week. They brought the house down."

Jane meets Jenelle's eye and raises a thin-pencilled eyebrow in her direction. "Really, you were there? And you never told me? I imagine they sounded great, though."

"You never answered my question, what about New Orleans? I'm serious, Jane."

"Really?"

"Yeah, of course?"

"You think I could make it over there? Would I be welcome in your community?"

Throwing both her hands up, Jenelle shakes her head. "Don't worry 'bout skin colour, it's not 'bout that, it's 'bout the music, the voice, the stage presence. All of which ya have, honey. Don't let the racial segregation shit get to ya."

Jane frowns, and Jenelle's delicate features mould into frustration.

Biting her lip, she admires her girlfriend's milk chocolate skin. The woman's jet-black hair, tied up in a red scarf with matching lipstick and red nails, accents her knockout looks.

"Hmm. I guess so. You're right, Jenelle."

"I am. Plus, Dr. Martin Luther King, he's doing all he can to help everyone move forward."

"Yeah, I guess so. Okay, let me give it some thought." Jane smiles, and her friend returns the gesture.

"You do that." Jenelle raises her martini. "I'd love

ya to come over." She clings her glass against Jane's as if to affirm a secret pact and vow of friendship.

Jane's attention drifts to the three men on stage, then lingers on the saxophonist playing an impromptu solo.

An hour later at the bar, alone and reflecting on her and Jenelle's plans to take over New Orleans together, Jane sips her drink slowly. She reminisces over the vivid dream of how the two of them would make a legacy together, as jazz and soul singers. In theory, every record label in the United States would offer sweet recording deals.

On a high over all the excitement, Jenelle took off with her date to Soho for a movie and a slice of pizza.

Staring into her martini glass, absent-minded, Jane detaches from the smokey atmosphere of Maurice's Place.

I can sing, that's about it, she muses, *that's all I know. Secretary, factory worker, seamstress . . . arrgh. These jobs are not for me.*

The lights dim slightly, ready for the next act to take the stage.

Looking across the room, Jane locks eyes with the handsome stranger playing the saxophone.

He smiles, and with the nod of his head, he tips his hat in her direction.

She shyly returns the gesture. A slight blush moves through her. Lowering her lashes, she empties the glass.

Oh, wow. That man.

The room stands still. It's as if everything flows in slow motion. Even long after the song ends, the melody, burned to memory, continues to sweep her way.

Raising her gaze in the band's direction, her eyes widen.

Where is he? She scans the room and finds who she's looking for.

Confidently, he strolls over to her with a smooth, easy glide to his gait.

She drinks him all in. He's easy on the eyes.

His pristine white shirt, black slim tie, milk chocolate skin, and beard, highlight his groomed-to-perfection look. He gives her another warm smile, then leans on the bar by her side.

"Evenin' Miss." Looking down at her sitting on a bar stool, he fixes Jane with a seductive gaze.

"Good evening. You were great up there."

"Thank ya, ma'am. Can I get ya another drink?"

"Sure, I'll take a martini, thanks. I never got your name?"

Holding out a hand to Jane, she puts her small palm in his.

"Louis." He places a kiss on the back of her knuckles. "Louis Simpson."

"Nice to meet you. I'm Jane O'Sullivan."

"You weren't too bad up there on stage ya'self. Ya really put a lot of heart into that last song."

"Thanks, I feel so at home on stage."

"Yeah, it shows."

"So, where are ya from? Not that I know a lot-a places in London. I just arrived a week ago."

"I'm from Shoreditch."

"Oh, yeah, the 'East-end', right? That's what you guys call it?"

"Sure is."

"I've not been over that way yet. I'm stayin' aroun' here just off Tottenham Court Road."

"Oh, nice, not a bad part of London at all, right in the centre."

"I heard a lot about the East-end though, some characters over there."

Jane pulls out another slim smoke and slides it into her long black holder.

"Allow me." Louis offers her a light, then takes out a smoke for himself from his pocket.

"Oh, you mean the Kray twins. They're crazy, all right. Just stay out of their way, that's all."

She laughs, fully aware of the reputation Ronnie and Reggie Kray have around London.

Two of the most formidable men in the East-end. The twins, loved by few but feared by many, create their fair share of trouble.

The bartender slides a martini glass, with a tumbler of whisky in front of her and Louis.

He pulls out a note from his wallet to pay, and Jane scrutinises him. His style, accent, smoothness, and confident body language speak to her in a way other men had failed to achieve.

"So, where are you from Louis? I know you're American, but what state?"

"Jackson, Mississippi."

"Wow, a true southerner."

"That's right, ma'am."

"So, how long have you been in the band?"

Louis glances over at his mates, Clive and Ray, at the other end of the bar where he left them, smoking and playing dominos.

"Ah, the boys, we've been together a lil' while now. 'Bout five years or so. We go way back. Grew up in Jackson, they're my buddies."

"Well, you guys are great together."

"Why, thank you, ma'am. So, this place is your gig? Ya sing here every week?"

"Sure do, two nights on stage and three serving cocktails."

Louis nods his head. "Nice place, welcoming.

Over here, me an' the boys ain't outsiders so much, if ya know what I mean?"

"Why's that?"

"Back in Jackson, ya don't see so much people mixin' together. The segregation is still there an' strong."

"Gosh, it's terrible. London's not perfect, but slowly things are changing with all the new people arriving from all over. Personally, I think it's wonderful."

"Let's toast to that, Miss."

Jane smiles warmly, then raises her glass to Louis.

"Talkin' 'bout mixing, do ya wanna dance?"

Jane beams back at Louis. "Yeah, I'd love to."

He guides her from the bar, over to the dance floor.

The sensation of eyes crawling over her—some in shock, some in admiration—makes a warmth spread across her cheeks and neck.

With his hand on the small of Jane's back, he glides her around the open space.

"Thank you, Louis."

"What for? I've not done anythin' to thank me for, yet."

Jane looks into Louis' handsome face. A wide grin stretches across his face from ear to ear.

His gentleman-like manners, southern accent,

and handsome face force the corners of her lips to curl.

"You have. Dancing is just what I needed to have a little fun and relax a bit. I love singing on stage, but it can overwhelm a person."

"Yeah, I understand that, ma'am. I know the feelin'. You go on an' relax now, don't worry 'bout the stage, you're with me."

He pulls Jane in closer and sways to the music.

All these people, all the stares. Mmm, I just met him, she thinks to herself. *Maybe this is wrong but . . .*

Something shifts internally for Jane, dousing the negative words floating in her head.

Why shouldn't I be happy? The thought makes her smile. *And why should I care what others think?*

Right now, his company equates to happiness. And she has every intention of getting to know this handsome southerner better.

5

IF YOU COULD DO IT AGAIN

London, 1985

The saxophone player changes his rhythm to an upbeat tune, and the melody cuts through the recesses of her thoughts.

Tightly closing, then opening her eyes, Jane blinks back the vivid memory from decades ago.

Oh, man, she says to herself, *focus already.*

The crowd, now doubled in size after her daydream, creates a barrier to block her view.

She can no longer see the musician from the bench, but every note he plays makes its way to her ears. With a few deep breaths, she regains her awareness that it's the 1980s not 1960s.

That was a long time ago, she scolds herself. *I need to move on.*

The crowd sways and dances in the middle of the busy street, distorting her focus on life and love.

Times have changed. Let it go and let him go.

Gathering her thoughts, she gets to her feet. Tears build in her eyes.

Determine to not allow them to ruin her evening, she blinks them back.

Jane makes her way toward Westminster Bridge, away from the crowd, then continues the journey home.

Her feet no longer pound the pavement or speed walk for exercise.

With a heavy heart, she weaves her way in and out of tourists and commuters and thinks back to another time.

He was quite a man back then, all those years ago in the swinging sixties. She contemplates.

She waits for a traffic light, crosses the street, then steps onto a sidewalk.

Is he even still alive? A sigh leaves her lips. *What is he doing with himself, is he married, or does he have children?*

Her mind whirls with a million questions, she has no way of ever finding the answers to.

All I know, she steps over a sprig of grass growing

though a crack in the concrete, *is that I loved him then, and deep down, I still do.*

Tears roll down her face, and she swipes at the clear, wet emotions of heartache.

He meant so much so to me, I'm sure I meant something to him too.

An hour later Jane walks into her home in Shoreditch, east London.

She kicks off her walking trainers in the narrow hallway, then strolls into her open-plan kitchen and living room.

Lilly, her daughter—now a fully-grown woman in her mid-twenties—waits for her. Six months ago, she and her boyfriend Jason had moved to the other side of east London to a more upmarket part for young up-and-coming professionals.

"Hi Mum, how was work?"

"Oh, hello, love." Jane stretches, allowing the tension in her neck to relax. "Nice to see you here." She pauses for dramatic effect. "I see you've moved out and left me but still held onto your door key."

"Mum, come on, not this again. I've not deserted you. I'm only a few miles away."

Walking farther into the kitchen to embrace Lilly, Jane sweeps her eyes over the kitchen. "Hmm, come here and give me a hug love. I'm just playing around. It's good to see you."

On the table, Jane notices the glossy holiday magazines shuffled around and out of their usual resting place.

"So, what's the plan now, Mum? You're a free woman. The world is your oyster."

"Let's get the kettle on first, then we'll talk about that."

"What's wrong? You don't seem yourself?"

"I'm fine, love. It's okay. Just a bit of an emotional day, really. I can't believe it. I've just retired."

"You sit down. Mum. I'll make the tea."

Jane does as she's told and slumps herself down at the glass kitchen table. Shifting her gaze to the magazines, she lets out a sigh.

Lilly fills the kettle with water. "What's up, Mum?"

"Nothing for you to worry about, honestly. Let's change the subject."

Lilly rolls her eyes in disbelief. "If you say so. Those flowers are lovely, let's get them in some water."

Jane waits at the table. "Sounds like a plan."

Lilly searches in the cupboards for a vase. "Tell me about your last day."

"Just grab a glass." Her mind floats to the farewell lunch, then to her last walk home.

"No. It's a special day for a special lady, and the occasion calls for the special vase."

"It was enjoyable, pretty crazy in fact."

The gas flame of the burner licks around the bottom of the kettle.

"How so?"

"I went to lunch with the entire team."

"Wait. Everyone?" Half of Lilly's body disappears behind a door.

"I've never felt so popular in all the years I've worked at that place."

"I'm sure they'll miss you. Twenty plus years is a long time to serve with an employer."

"Yeah, I'll miss them too."

"You will. But this is a new stage of life now, one for you to enjoy. I see you've got some holiday magazines. It's time to get out there. See what life has to offer."

"Did you move it—the vase, Mum? I don't see it."

"It's on the left next to the soufflé dish."

Picking up a magazine from the table, Jane thumbs through it. Images of females with the afterglow of warmer weather and tanned skin, grace the pages.

"Found it." Lilly arranges the long stem flowers in the vase.

"I have no idea where to go. I could do with a bit of sun."

"Exactly, that's more like it. Are you thinking of the Mediterranean? I flicked through your magazines. It looks like paradise."

Lilly, standing by the sink, chews anxiously on the inner corner of her lip.

"Yes, it looks lovely. Well, the magazines make it look engaging, anyway. Only thing is, I'll be on my own."

Once upon a time, she had agreed to travel, her and a friend.

Her mind wanders through time, back to 1960, and stops at the conversation she had with Jenelle at Maurice's Place—the same night Louis had walked into her life.

The vivid conservation she had with Jenelle so long ago, causes her heart to become as heavy as a ton of bricks. Her breathing shallows at the memories—good, bad, and indifferent.

"That's half the adventure and fun. You'll make new friends." A long, dramatised sigh leaves her daughter's lips. "I had a feeling you were going to use that as an excuse."

Lilly's voice pulls her out of her thoughts.

"I had so many ideas of what I'd do once retirement came around, but now, I find myself empty-handed."

Lilly places the vase on the table, then lowers her face to hers. "I've got something to show you. But let me make the tea first."

Returning to the kettle, Lilly pours steaming water into the cups to steep the tea.

Jane admires her daughter's profile from behind. Tall and slender in stature, with a mass of curly dark brown ringlets falling to her shoulders.

She sure is a pretty girl, with her father's features.

Her full lips and large hazel eyes remind her of him each time she looks into her face.

Jane smiles at Lilly's fashionable leggings and bright t-shirt.

"Careful, it's hot, Mum."

"Got it." Jane rotates the cup, so she can grab the handle with her right hand, then picks it up.

Her daughter returns to the table with two mugs of hot tea, sets them down, then reaches under the table and into her bag.

"Keep an opened mind." A folded, worn article from a Sunday paper's free magazine insert rests in her hand.

"What do you think of this?" Lilly places the article on the table. "No excuses about travelling on your own."

Jane sets her mug on the table surface, then picks up the announcement.

The article's page looks just like the glossy magazines on the table. Bright images of paradise beaches, delicious foods, and a beautiful-looking cruise ship jump off the page.

Silver Fox Tours, she reads to herself. *Mediterranean Cruise, £1,700.*

"Well?" Lilly's eyes hold a treasure trove of hope.

"Silver Fox." A sigh escapes her lips, then she chews on the £1,700.

Is that what I am now? A Silver Fox? Silver as in grey and old?

"You always said you wanted to travel again. This is the perfect opportunity."

"Discover islands of pure beauty," she projects her voice, adding a bit of theatrical flair to her words. "Come and set sail on a seven-or three-day cruise. You'll relax in the sun as you sail across the deep blue waters of the Mediterranean."

"You said you needed some sun." A grin stretches across Lilly's lips.

"Guests will have the opportunity to tour and explore ancient parts of Greece, picturesque villages, stunning markets, and paradise beaches across the Mediterranean."

"Just think of the sightseeing and the people

you'll meet." She scoots her chair closer. "Where do they dock midway through?"

"Says here, *'The ship will then head to Turkey at the mid-point of the cruise where you will find some remarkable beaches, scenery, and culture.'* And it seems throughout the trip, they'll serve mouth-watering Mediterranean dishes three times a day."

"See, no cooking. As a guest, you can relax and enjoy the views and sun on deck. Check out their complimentary amenities. I recall reading something about top of the range gyms, saunas, pools, spa treatments, and"—she wiggles her brows—"unisex salons."

"That ship left port and sailed long ago."

"Mum, you're not dead, so live a little." She sips her tea. "They even have an old Hollywood inspired casino on board. Evening entertainment includes live bands and performances. And I know how much you enjoy listening to music."

"I'll think about it."

"The cruise will take you to a warm and vibrant part of the world. So, instead of bundling up here at home because of the cold, you can enjoy the sunshine."

"I don't know about this, Lilly. I'd be alone with a bunch of people—strangers."

"All in their forties and fifties, singles and

couples. You'll find the cruise dates on the back." She taps the brochure. "The ship departs from Dover or Birmingham.".

— 1st August - 7th August - Dover: Venus and Empress cruise ship

— 9th- 16th August - Dover: Victoria cruise ship

— 18th-24th August - Birmingham: Diana cruise ship

—26th-1st September - Birmingham: Duchess cruise ship

"I'm not so sure about—"

"Oh, go on, Mum." Lilly's hazel eyes, bright and hopeful, say it all. "Live a little and don't give me that look."

Remaining mute, Jane swallows hard and stares blankly at her daughter.

"Mum." Softening her tone, Lilly liberates the papers from Jane's grasp, then wraps her fingers around her mother's hands.

Travelling again sounds nice, but the thought of going it alone makes her feel so alone.

"This is a splendid chance to get out there, don't you see? All your life, you've worked hard. Provided for us, and you've even gone without because you were on your own with me. Now's your chance to take back something for yourself. Please say yes."

"Hmm."

"When you were my age, what was your dream? What did you hope for?"

"When I was your age, Lilly, I had dreams just like you. But life changed, it had to love."

"Exactly my point, if you could do it all again, what would you do?"

Sighing, Jane shakes her head. "Can't go back. Time doesn't work that way. But if I could, I wouldn't change a thing."

"Anyway, I just wanted to stop by and congratulate you on your newfound freedom, and let you know Saturday night, we're taking you out. No excuses. A nice dinner with me and Jason."

"No need for all that, love, honestly I–"

"Too late, it's all booked." Lilly gets to her feet and beams warmly. "Come 'er, Mum. Love you, see you on Saturday."

Jane wraps her arms around Lilly, embracing her in a loving hug. Her eyes well with tears, which she tries to hide.

"Thanks, love, see you soon."

"Bye, Mum."

Later that night, Jane fills the bathtub with bubbles. She lights some scented candles, pours herself a glass of red wine, then she loads her cassette player with her favourite tape.

Soft instrumental jazz fills the room.

The full-bodied sound of a saxophone playing a jazzy version of *Ain't No Sunshine When She's Gone*, makes a smile break out across her lips.

Pinning her hair up, then undressing, she takes in her naked reflection in the mirror.

Everything changes, she thinks with a sigh. *I'm hardly the same woman I once was.*

Her body has aged gracefully, she did her best not to let herself go too much over the years.

No regrets, everything happens for a reason. Even if life never panned out how I expected.

Her decision to keep Lilly even though it was a hard choice to make is a decision she's glad she made. The truth of the matter, if she hadn't kept Lilly, over the years, she doubted she could have carried on persisting to make the life she had dreamed of. The life she dreamed of before she conceived Lilly.

It's not that she was maternal at the time she conceived, circumstances and instinct naturally made it hard for her to rid her body of her child.

She blows out an impatient breath, then moves her gaze away from the mirror.

The relaxing bath calls to her.

Easing herself in steamy warmth, her body adjusts to the temperature. Her mind drifts off again in a daydream with the soft music and candlelight as her only company.

"Louis." The name rolls off her lips. "The drug my body is still addicted to."

6

HOPEFUL

Maurice's Place, London, 1960

Toasting Louis' glass, Jane sighs with a faraway look in her eyes as if daydreaming. "I'm really pleased to hear all about the civil rights movement back home, Louis."

"Yeah, like I said, segregation, it's still there but, work is bein' done. That's somethin' to be thankful for."

Louis' voice seems to snap her out of her distant thoughts, and the corners of her lips tug into a small smile.

"What's on ya mind, ma'am? Looks like someone's told a joke I never got to hear."

"Oh, nothing, sorry I was just . . . it doesn't matter, honestly." Lowering her gaze, Jane blushes.

Smiling, he studies her closely. Her blonde back-combed hair, held in place with a white scarf, and her heavily lined eyes, draw him in. Her beauty is just as alluring as her singing voice.

"I'm not one to pry but if somethin' is on your mind—"

"—I'm fine." She rests a hand lightly on Louis' shoulder. "Honestly, I'm okay. I was just thinking about a conversation I had with Jenelle that's all."

"What's botherin' ya?"

"Oh, nothing in particular, I'm excited about the future, that's all, especially now I've heard about the progress being made from you."

"All right, Miss, then I guess we got nothin' ta worry 'bout."

Draining his tumbler of whisky, Louis signals for another drink. "What time ya finishin' up tonight?"

"I'm done now."

"I got another couple of numbers to play, then we're done for the night too." He takes a step, then stops. "Don't go anywhere, I'll be right back, that is, if ya don't mind waitin' on me?"

"It's not like I got anywhere to go, I'll be here."

"I'll walk ya home if that's not too forward? I

don't know British mannerisms, and I don't wanna overstep the line, ma'am."

Louis' eyes flash over Jane from head to toe, and she blushes, then drains her martini glass.

"That would be nice, Louis. I'd like that."

Giving her a wink, his attention turns to the bartender.

"One for the lady too, please." Reaching in his pocket, he extracts his wallet and pulls out a note.

Louis examines the unfamiliar currency, hoping what's in hand covers the total.

Jane smiles at his profile, watching him fumble around with the note.

The bar tender places a fresh martini glass in front of her, and Louis hands over the payment.

"I'll be right back, don't go anywhere." Pocketing the change, he makes his way through the crowd to Clive and Ray.

www.ingramcontent.com/pod-product-compliance
Lightning Source LLC
Chambersburg PA
CBHW060318050426
42449CB00011B/2546